WILLIAM W

The Story of his Life,

WITH CRITICAL REMARKS ON HIS WRITINGS.

BY

JAMES MIDDLETON SUTHERLAND.

1887

To

William Wordsworth

"Mr. Wordsworth . . . had a dignified manner, with a deep and roughish but not unpleasing voice, and an exalted mode of speaking. He had a habit of keeping his left hand in the bosom of his waistcoat; and in this attitude, except when he turned round to take one of the subjects of his criticism from the shelves (for his contemporaries were there also), he sat dealing forth his eloquent but hardly catholic judgments. . . . Walter Scott said that the eyes of Burns were the finest he ever saw. I cannot say the same of Mr. Wordsworth; that is, not in the sense of the beautiful, or even of the profound. But certainly I never beheld eyes which looked so inspired and supernatural. They were like fires half burning, half smouldering with a sort of acrid fixture of regard, and seated at the further end of two caverns. One might imagine Ezekiel or Isaiah to have had such eyes. The finest eyes, in every sense of the word, which I have ever seen in a man's head (and I have seen many fine ones), are those of Thomas Carlyle."—1815.

An Excerpt from
The Autobiography of Leigh Hunt, 1850
By Leigh Hunt

". . . He (Wordsworth) talked well in his way; with veracity, easy brevity, and force, as a wise tradesman would of his tools and workshop,—and as no unwise one could. His voice was good, frank, and sonorous, though practically clear, distinct, and forcible, rather than melodious; the tone of him business-like, sedately confident; no discourtesy, yet no anxiety about being courteous.

A fine wholesome rusticity, fresh as his mountain breezes, sat well on the stalwart veteran, and on all he said and did. You would have said he was a usually taciturn man; glad to unlock himself to audience sympathetic and intelligent when such offered itself.

His face bore marks of much, not always peaceful, meditation; the look of it not bland or benevolent so much as close, impregnable, and hard: a man *multa tacere loquive paratus*, in a world where he had experienced no lack of contradictions as he strode along! The eyes were not very brilliant, but they had a quiet clearness; there was enough of brow, and well-shaped; rather too much of cheek ('horse face' I have heard satirists say); face of squarish shape, and decidedly longish, as I think the head itself was (its 'length' going horizontal); he was large-boned, lean, but still firm-knit, tall, and strong-looking when he stood, a right good old steel-gray figure, with rustic simplicity and dignity about him, and a vivacious strength looking through him which might have suited one of those old steel-gray markgrafs whom Henry the Fowler set up to ward the 'marches' and do battle with the heathen in a stalwart and judicious manner."

AN EXCERPT FROM
Reminiscences, 1881
BY THOMAS CARLYLE

"His features were large, and not suddenly expressive; they conveyed little idea of the 'poetic fire' usually associated with brilliant imagination. His eyes were mild and up-looking, his mouth coarse rather than refined, his forehead high rather than broad; but every action seemed considerate, and every look self-possessed, while his voice, low in tone, had that persuasive eloquence which invariably 'moves men.'"—1832.

AN EXCERPT FROM
Memories of Great Men. . . , 1871
BY ANNA MARIA HALL

PREFACE.

In issuing this unpretending volume on William Wordsworth, I need offer but few prefatory remarks.

Whilst there are, as is well known, several indispensable hand-books on this great meditative poet, all more or less elaborate and exhaustive in their way, there is, perhaps, none that is precisely what this professes to be—a popular story of his life; and it is in the hope of supplying one, however humble, that this condensed monograph, the writing of which has indeed been a labour of love, is given to the public.

The 'Memoirs of William Wordsworth,' by the poet's nephew, the Right Rev. Christopher Wordsworth, D.D., late Lord Bishop of Lincoln, and the

'Biography,' by the late Rev. E. Paxton Hood, are daily becoming more scarce, having long been out of print, and there would appear to be little likelihood that publications of such magnitude will be re-issued; and it is believed that many will find leisure to peruse this brief sketch who would, doubtless, be deterred from reading volumes of greater length and merit.

'Poets,' it has been well said, 'are the unacknowledged legislators of the world,' and the name of Wordsworth has grown to be a power in the land that even he in his most ambitious moments never could have anticipated; whilst his influence on the spirit of the age, and on readers of all kinds—perhaps more especially on the young—is simply incalculable. To know something, therefore, of such a man, is not only essential, but desirable to a degree; and the present work, within its limited compass, contains, in general at least, accurate and comprehensive information on, at all events, the leading incidents in his prolonged and truly honourable career.

Wordsworth is not the poet of passion and sentiment, but rather—and this is his praise—of reflection, purity, and humanity; and it is good at times, particularly in these nineteenth-century days of life-at-high-pressure—when, in the words of Pope, we have 'too much thinking to have common thought'—for man to be alone; to withdraw himself at intervals from his fellows; and to commune with Nature and with his own heart.

I have to acknowledge my deep indebtedness to a large number of authorities, too extensive to mention in a preface; and if I have inadvertently made use of any copyright matter without the necessary permission, I must ask those interested to accept the expression of my unfeigned regret, and to grant their kind indulgence. I have not wilfully trespassed in this respect. To F. W. H. Myers, Esq., author of the excellent volume on *Wordsworth*, published in the *English Men of Letters Series*, I have to avow my hearty and special thanks for his cheerful consent to give the extract from the important letter of Dorothy Wordsworth, with reference to 'The White Doe of Rylstone,' and any others I might require to make.

PREFACE.

I desire also to embrace this—the earliest—opportunity of publicly thanking most cordially Miss Quillinan, of Loughrigg Holme, Rydal; the Rev. Henry M. Fletcher, rector of Grasmere; J. Fleming Green, Esq., of Grasmere; and Robert Crewdson, Esq., of Rydal Mount; for their generous kindness, and for the valuable assistance afforded by one and all, during my recent visit to the Lake District.

If the perusal of this biography lead to any of its readers making or renewing their acquaintance with the imperishable writings of the poet, and impart but a tithe of the pleasure experienced by me in its composition, I shall accomplish the objects I had in view throughout, and be more than abundantly rewarded.

> ' He either fears his fate too much,
> Or his deserts are small,
> Who dares not put it to the touch,
> To win or lose it all.'

J. M. S.

November, 1887.

AT THE GRAVE OF WORDSWORTH.

(November 9, 1887.)

THE world is sadly short such hearts as thine,
   High Priest in Nature's temple, now at rest ;
   Among thy lovers do I stand confest ;
Thy lays, a glorious legacy, are mine.
In thee I see a genius half divine,
   A man that loved his fellow-men sincere ;
   In purpose fixed and strong, in vision clear ;
Singer at once and sage—in feeling fine.
Tho' dead thou speakest, noble minstrel, seer ;
   For thy inspiring verse no more can die
     Than can thy spirit gone to God who gave.
Accept my homage as I linger here,
   Between thy sacred ashes and the sky,
     And humbly place this wreath upon thy grave.

CONTENTS.

CONTENTS.

CONTENTS.

CHAPTER VI.

CHAPTER VII.

CHAPTER VIII.

CHAPTER IX.

CONTENTS.

WILLIAM WORDSWORTH:

THE STORY OF HIS LIFE.

~~~

CHAPTER I.

> ' At first, the infant,
> Mewling and puking in the nurse's arms.
> And then the whining school-boy, with his satchel,
> And shining morning face, creeping like snail
> Unwillingly to school.'
>
> *Shakespeare.*

Some tributes to Wordsworth's eminence as a poet—His birth (April 7, 1770) and parentage—His mother dies (1778)—Is sent to the Grammar School, Hawkshead, where he makes his first attempts at poetry—His impressions of his mother—Early days at Penrith and Cockermouth—His youthful pastimes described—His father dies (1783)—Is sent to Cambridge (Oct., 1787)—Does not like the restraint of university life—Studies Italian and the earlier English poets—Enjoys life at the university—Spends his first summer vacation in the Vale of Esthwaite—His self-dedication to Nature—Writes 'An Evening Walk,' etc.—In 1790, his last vacation, makes a tour through France, Switzerland, and the North of Italy—Takes his B.A. degree (Jan., 1791), and quits the university.

IT has been well said, ' What a glorious gift God bestows on a nation when He gives them a poet;'

1

and William Wordsworth is, by common consent, one of the brightest stars in the firmament of English literature. Let us be quite clear, in starting, upon this point.

Southey says of him : ‘A greater poet than Wordsworth there never has been, nor ever will be.’ ‘Two or three generations must pass before the public affect to admire such poets as Milton and Wordsworth. Of such men the world scarcely produces one in a millennium.’ Wilson, in one of his masterly essays, thus writes of him : ‘We believe that Wordsworth's genius has now a greater influence on the spirit of poetry in Britain than was ever exercised by any individual mind. He was the first man who impregnated all his descriptions of external nature with sentiment and passion. . . . He was the first man that vindicated the native dignity of human nature, by showing that all her elementary feelings were capable of poetry —and in that, too, he has been followed by other true poets, although here he stands, and probably ever will stand, unapproached. He was the first man that stripped thought and passion of all vain or foolish disguises, and showed them in their just proportions and unencumbered power. He was the first man who, in poetry, knew the real province of language, and suffered it not to veil the meanings of the spirit. In all these things—and in many more — Wordsworth is indisputably the most

original poet of the age ; and it is impossible in the
very nature of things that he ever can be eclipsed.'
'Mr. Wordsworth,' says Hazlitt, 'is the most
original poet now living. . . . His poetry is not
external, but internal ; it does not depend upon
tradition, or story, or old song ; he furnishes it
from his own mind, and is his own subject. . . .
Of many of the Lyrical Ballads, it is not possible to
speak in terms of too high praise. . . . They open
a finer and deeper vein of thought and feeling than
any poet in modern times has done, or attempted.'
Coleridge writes : ' I speak with heartfelt sincerity,
and, I think, unblinded judgment, when I tell you
that I feel myself a little man by his side. . . .'
And, again : 'The giant Wordsworth—God-love
him ! . . . He has written near twelve hundred
lines of blank verse, superior, I hesitate not to aver,
to anything in our language which any way resembles it.' And, lastly, to be brief, William
Ellery Channing says : ' The great poet of our
times, Wordsworth—one of the few who are to live
—has gone to common life, to the feelings of our
universal nature, to the obscure and neglected portions of society, for beautiful and touching themes.
Genius is not a creator, in the sense of fancying or
feigning what does not exist. Its distinction is to
discern more of truth than common minds. It sees
under disguises and humble forms everlasting beauty.
. . . Wordsworth is the poet of humanity ; he

teaches reverence for our universal nature; he breaks down the factitious barriers between human hearts.'

William Wordsworth, the greatest metaphysical and philosophical poet that England has ever produced, was born at Cockermouth, in Cumberland, on the 7th of April, 1770, the year of Chatterton's melancholy death. He was the second son of John Wordsworth, attorney-at-law, and law-agent to Sir James Lowther, first Earl of Lonsdale. His mother, whose Christian name was Anne, was the only daughter of William Cookson, a mercer of Penrith. Both his parents came of ancient families, and that of his father could be traced back to before the Conquest. The poet was the second of five children —four sons and one daughter. His earliest years were spent between Cockermouth and Penrith, where his mother died in 1778. He thus alludes to her removal :

> 'Early died
> My honoured mother, she who was the heart
> And hinge of all our learnings and our loves.
> She left us destitute.'

She 'died of a decline, brought on by a cold, the consequence of being put, at a friend's house in London, in what used to be called "a best bed-room."' In 1778, he was sent, with his brother Richard, to the Grammar School, at Hawkshead, in Lancashire, where his first attempts at poetry, in which he afterwards became so famous, were made.

His father, who never got over the death of the poet's mother, died in 1783. He was thus left an orphan before he had completed his fourteenth year. His impressions of his parents, therefore, could not have been very defined, which is greatly to be regretted, as he would otherwise, doubtless, have referred to them in his poems more fully than he has done.

'I remember my mother,' he says, 'only in some few situations, one of which was her pinning a nosegay to my breast when I was going to say the catechism in the church, as was customary before Easter. I remember also telling her on one week-day that I had been at church, for our school stood in the churchyard, and we had frequent opportunities of seeing what was going on there. The occasion was, a woman doing penance in the church in a white sheet. My mother commended my having been present, expressing a hope that I should remember the circumstance for the rest of my life.

'"But," said I, "mamma, they did not give me a penny, as I had been told they would."

'"Oh!" said she, recanting her praises, "if that was your motive, you were very properly disappointed."

'My last impression was having a glimpse of her on passing the door of her bedroom during her last illness, when she was reclining in her easy-chair.

An intimate friend of hers, Miss Hamilton 1
name, who was used to visit her at Cockermout
told me that she once said to her, that the only o
of her five children about whose future life she w
anxious, was William; and he, she said, would
remarkable either for good or for evil. The cau
of this was, that I was of a stiff, moody, ai
violent temper; so much so that I remember goi
once into the attics of my grandfather's house
Penrith, upon some indignity having been put up
me, with an intention of destroying myself wi
one of the foils which I knew was kept there.
took the foil in hand, but my heart failed. Up
another occasion, while I was at my grandfathe
house at Penrith, along with my eldest broth
Richard, we were whipping tops together in t
large drawing-room, on which the carpet was oi
laid down upon particular occasions. The wa
were hung round with family pictures, and I said
my brother:

' " Dare you strike your whip through that (
lady's petticoat ?"

' He replied :

' " No ; I won't."

' " Then," said I, " here goes ;" and I struck 1
lash through her hooped petticoat, for which,
doubt, though I have forgotten it, I was prope:
punished. But, possibly from some want of ju(
ment in punishments inflicted, I had become p

verse and obstinate in defying chastisement, and rather proud of it than otherwise.

'Of my earliest days at school I have little to say, but that they were very happy ones, chiefly because I was left at liberty, then and in the vacations, to read whatever books I liked. For example, I read all Fielding's works, "Don Quixote," "Gil Blas," and any part of Swift that I liked; "Gulliver's Travels," and the "Tale of the Tub," being both much to my taste. . . . It may be, perhaps, as well to mention, that the first verses which I wrote were a task imposed by my master; the subject, "The Summer Vacation;" and of my own accord I added others upon "Return to School." There was nothing remarkable in either poem; but I was called upon, among other scholars, to write verses upon the completion of the second centenary from the foundation of the school in 1585, by Archbishop Sandys. These verses were much admired, far more than they deserved, for they were but a tame imitation of Pope's versification, and a little in his style.'

We attach no slight importance to the foregoing account of the poet's early life, inasmuch as he himself tells us, that 'the child is father of the man;' and this was pre-eminently true in his own case. Like Cowper, he lost his mother, who was a woman of amiable, pious, and affectionate disposition, when he was very young; and her decease, coupled with that of his father, must naturally

have exercised a chastening, if not a depressing
effect upon his character. Wide and varied as are
the subjects upon which Wordsworth wrote, we
search in vain for any trace of the comic element in
his verse. Whatever else he was, therefore, he was
not a mirth-provoking poet ; his ideal of poetry was
higher and more spiritual.

Cockermouth, the poet's birthplace, which is
thirteen miles distant from Keswick, the most
beautifully-situated town in England, stands near
the banks of the Derwent, and was in every way
favourable to the development of his poetic genius.
Having received the rudiments of education at
Penrith at a dame's school, where he had as class-
mate a little girl of the name of Mary Hutchinson,
his own cousin, he spent a year or two at Cockermouth, under the tuition of the Reverend Mr. Gil-
banks. What pleasant rambles the poet in embryo
must have had by the side of the ' bright blue river,'
which he subsequently so greatly celebrated ! He
alludes, in feeling language, to its influence upon
him, in the following lines :

> ' One, the fairest of all rivers, loved
> To blend his murmurs with my nurse's song,
> And, from his alder shades and rocky falls,
> And from his fords and shallows, sent a voice
> That flowed along my dreams.'

The town is one of some antiquity, with its
dismantled baronial castle and broken battlements ;
and it is interesting to know that the house in

which Wordsworth was born is still standing. It faces the principal street, whilst its garden runs down to the verge of the river. His father's remains repose in the churchyard. In his delightful autobiographical poem, 'The Prelude,' the poet refers at some length to his reminiscences of Cockermouth and Hawkshead. He tells us, how, many a time, when but five years old, he 'made one long bathing of a summer's day,' in a mill-race; how, before he was ten, he used in winter

> 'To range the open heights where woodcocks run
> Along the smooth green turf;'

how, in the spring, he loved to go plundering the raven's nest, at the imminent risk of his life; and how, one summer evening, prompted by nature, he stealthily entered a boat which he found moored by the lake of Esthwaite to a willow-tree, and, unloosing the chain, rowed off in triumph. The passage in which he narrates what followed, is one of the finest in his writings, and must, in part, be cited:

> 'Like one who rows,
> Proud of his skill, to reach a chosen point
> With an unswerving line, I fixed my view
> Upon the summit of a craggy ridge,
> The horizon's utmost boundary; far above
> Was nothing but the stars and the gray sky.
> She was an elfin pinnace; lustily
> I dipped my oars into the silent lake,
> And, as I rose upon the stroke, my boat
> Went heaving through the water like a swan;
> When, from behind that craggy steep till then

The horizon's bound, a huge peak, black and huge,
As if with voluntary power instinct
Upreared its head.   I struck and struck again,
And growing still in stature the grim shape
Towered up between me and the stars, and still,
For so it seemed, with purpose of its own
And measured motion like a living thing,
Strode after me.'

His experiences as a skater are graphically given
in a spirited outburst of verse, which has been
quoted and admired times without number.   His
nutting and fishing expeditions, together with his
' unfading recollections ' of kite-flying, are also
gracefully referred to.   Those must have been
golden days at Hawkshead ; and the picturesque
scenery amidst which he strayed must have equipped
him with many never-to-be-forgotten pictures, hung
in the brightest gallery of his memory, to furnish
poems in the after-time.

Much of his poetical tendency, we think, must be
attributed to his father, who was a man of strong
and vigorous mind, and possessed of considerable
eloquence, and who gave him, at a very early age,
portions of the best English poets to be learned by
heart, with the gratifying result that he could,
when yet a boy, repeat many of the choicest passages
in Spenser, Shakespeare, and Milton.

By the death of his father, which, as we have
incidentally stated, occurred in 1783, the prospects
of the family were greatly clouded, the Earl of
Lonsdale being indebted to him to the extent

of some five thousand pounds, for cash advanced and professional services. All attempts to recover the money during the lifetime of this remarkable peer proved hopelessly futile; and when it is mentioned that this amount represented the bulk of the property of the family, some idea of their position may be gathered. It remains to be recorded, that the debt was not discharged until 1802, nineteen years afterwards, when the second Earl, eager to make amends for the unfeeling conduct of his father, liquidated the same, with interest, by a payment of £8,500.

In October. 1787. Wordsworth. being in his eighteenth year, was sent by his uncles, Richard Wordsworth and Christopher Crackanthorpe, who were also his guardians, to St. John's College, Cambridge, where he remained rather more than three years. His impressions on his arrival, and during his residence, are fully described in 'The Prelude,' and were, perhaps, upon the whole, pretty much what might be expected in the case of one who had been born and bred among the mountains. Poet-like, he did not take very kindly to the restraint of university life, and he made, generally speaking, little progress in the higher mathematics. But he made great advances in learning of other kinds. He read the classics diligently, and studied Italian and the earlier English poets — notably Chaucer, Spenser, Shakespeare, and Milton. He

was a dreamer, and, consequently, but a desultory
reader. The remembrance of his early years, spent
amid the beautifully-varied scenery of the Lake
District, was ever present with him ; ' the sounding
cataract,' ' the tall rock, the mountain, and the
deep and gloomy wood, their colours and their
forms '—all these haunted him like a passion.

He entered heartily into the pleasures of university
life, however :

> ' Companionships,
> Friendships, acquaintances, were welcome all.
> We sauntered, played, or rioted ; we talked
> Unprofitable talk at morning hours ;
> Drifted about along the streets and walks,
> Read lazily in trivial books, went forth
> To gallop through the country in blind zeal
> Of senseless horsemanship, or on the breast
> Of Cam sailed boisterously, and let the stars
> Come forth, perhaps without one quiet thought.'

He had a deep sense of the sacredness of the
university—' that garden of great intellects '—and
he could not lightly pass to and fro through the
gateways, or sleep in the chambers, with which so
many of the illustrious dead were associated. It so
happened that one of his college friends was domiciled
in ' the very room honoured by Milton's name,' and it
is a notable fact that Wordsworth, ' one of a festive
circle,' drank copious libations of wine to the
memory of the departed bard, to such a degree that,
for the first and last time in his life, he became—
may we not say under the circumstances ?—rap-
turously, but excusably, inebriated. We yield to

none in our love and heartfelt reverence for Wordsworth, and our object in thus recording what
some might, perhaps, be inclined to wish had been
omitted, is simply to show—but that strongly—that
he was a man of like passions with ourselves,
subject, too, to temptation as we are, and not
without sin.　Near his rooms in the university, he
tells us :

> ' Hung Trinity's loquacious clock,
> Who never let the quarters, night or day,
> Slip by him unproclaimed, and told the hours
> Twice over with a male and female voice.
> Her pealing organ was my neighbour too ;
> And from my pillow, looking forth by light
> Of moon or favouring stars, I could behold
> The antechapel where the statue stood
> Of Newton with his prism and silent face,
> The marble index of a mind for ever
> Voyaging through strange seas of thought, alone.'

Wordsworth's university career, as may be inferred,
grievously disappointed his friends, and not, perhaps,
without sufficient reason ; since, instead of applying
himself with all his mind, and with all his strength,
to his studies, with the view of gaining the highest
academic honours, he passed his time ' in vague and
loose indifference.' Yet who can wonder at it ?　He
was but ' a stripling of the hills,' and had been
brought up, particularly since the death of his
parents, in a delightful state of liberty ; he had
never passed through any of the great public schools;
and, moreover, with regard to the university, he had
a feeling that he ' was not for that hour, nor for

that place.' He spent his first summer vacation, not, as he might have done, amongst his books, but in the beautiful Vale of Esthwaite. And, no doubt, it was well that he did so, since prolonged absence from the scenes he prized so deeply might have caused his love for them to diminish. With what enthusiasm he renewed his acquaintance with Nature in his beloved regions, can be better imagined than described—

> 'When first I made
> Once more the circuit of our little lake,
> If ever happiness hath lodged with man,
> That day consummate happiness was mine,
> Wide-spreading, steady, calm, contemplative.'

He occupied the very bed in which he had been accustomed to sleep during his school-days. And now occurred an incident that shaped the course of his after-life. He had devoted the night to dancing and gaiety—

> ''Mid a throng
> Of maids and youths, old men, and matrons staid,
> A medley of all tempers'—

and was returning at daybreak, when a sunrise of extraordinary splendour and magnificence burst upon his enraptured vision, and melted his very soul. A more glorious spectacle he had never beheld.

> 'My heart was full; I made no vows, but vows
> Were then made for me; bond unknown to me
> Was given, that I should be, else sinning greatly,
> A dedicated spirit. On I walked
> In thankful blessedness, which yet survives.'

We love to think of the happy hours enjoyed by the youthful Wordsworth, after the seclusion of college life, in the beguiling company of the 'frank-hearted maids of rocky Cumberland.'

It is somewhat remarkable that, although he remained four sessions at Cambridge, he wrote but little verse; indeed, he produced only one or two poems. It was here that 'An Evening Walk' was composed; the scenery depicted, however, is not that round about Cambridge, as might be presumed, but that of the fascinating haunts of his youth. But of this poem more anon. Here, too, he penned the 'Lines written while sailing in a boat at evening.' The influence of the university was unmistakably anti-poetic, and 'froze the genial current of his soul.'

The several vacations were passed by Wordsworth in various parts of the country; but during the last one, that of 1790, he made a pedestrian tour with an esteemed fellow-collegian, Robert Jones, a Welshman, afterwards a clergyman of the Church of England, through France, Switzerland, and the North of Italy. 'We went,' he tells us, 'staff in hand, without knapsacks, and carrying each his needments tied up in a pocket-handkerchief, with about £20 apiece in our pockets.' They crossed from Dover and landed at Calais on the 13th of July, 1790, the eve of the memorable day on which the King—Louis XVI.—took the oath of fidelity to the New Constitution ; and there they saw,

> ' In a mean city, and among a few,
> How bright a face is worn when joy of one
> Is joy for tens of millions.'

After an absence of about fourteen weeks, they returned to England.

In January, 1791, having taken his degree of B.A., Wordsworth quitted the university.

CHAPTER II.

'There's a divinity that shapes our ends,
Rough-hew them how we will.'

Shakespeare.

Wordsworth makes a tour in North Wales — Is urged to enter the Church—His misgivings—He revisits France (Nov., 1791) during the Revolution—His sympathy with the movement—Becomes a patriot—Associates with the military officers in Paris — Forms a friendship with Beaupuis at Orleans—Proceeds thence to Blois—Returns to Paris, and finds France a Republic—Hears Robespierre denounced—Is compelled to return to England—Is again urged to embrace the clerical profession — Obstacles in the way—Deplores the results of the Revolution—Is opposed to the Bar—Annoyance of his relatives—'An Evening Walk' (1793)—'Descriptive Sketches' (1793)—Visits the Isle of Wight, where Raisley Calvert lies ill—Spends his time afterwards in visiting his friends—His dreary prospects—Contemplates starting the *Philanthropist* —Hears of the fall of Robespierre—His thankfulness thereupon—Is reduced to extremity, and seeks employment on the Metropolitan press—Raisley Calvert dies, and leaves him £900 (1795)—Is restored to the companionship of his sister Dorothy.

AFTER leaving Cambridge, and spending about four months in London, Wordsworth made a tour on foot through North Wales, with his friend Jones ; and, if we may judge from some of the sights they saw, the excursion must indeed have been an enjoy-

2

able one. We can picture to ourselves the ' two travellers plodding slowly along the road side by side,
each with his little knapsack of necessaries upon his
shoulders.' Wordsworth especially must have drank
in the beauty and grandeur of the scenery through
which they passed, and he refers, in a dedicatory
epistle to his fellow-traveller, to ' the sea-sunsets,
which give such splendour to the Vale of Clwyd,
Snowdon, the Chair of Idris, the quiet village of
Bethgelert, Menai and her Druids, the Alpine steeps
of the Conway, and the still more interesting wind-
ings of the wizard stream of the Dee.'

About this time the influence of his relatives was
brought to bear upon him with regard to entering
the Church, but he was not yet of age for ordination. He had grave misgivings, moreover, as to
his general fitness for holy orders, as we shall
see presently; and, without making up his mind
respecting his future career, in November, 1791, he
again set out for France. On this occasion he
travelled alone. He made his way to Paris, and
remained there some little time; but he soon
quitted it for Orleans, where he might be more
retired, for the purpose of studying the language.
His stay in France extended to some thirteen
months, during which period he witnessed much that
he could never forget. Those were stirring times.
The Revolution was raging far and wide like a
tempest. Wordsworth, like most youthful poets

—Coleridge and Southey amongst the number—was a violent republican, and he hailed the event with feelings of intense ardour, looking forward to the advent of a new and glorious era of liberty and happiness to mankind.　No wonder, therefore, that he, in all the enthusiasm of poetic fervour, allowed himself to be sucked into the vortex of the political excitement.　It would have been more remarkable had he escaped the danger.

> '"Twas in truth an hour
> Of universal ferment ; mildest men
> Were agitated ; and commotions, strife
> Of passion and opinion, filled the walls
> Of peaceful houses with unquiet sounds.
> The soil of common life was, at that time,
> Too hot to tread upon.'

He had welcomed the inception of the Revolution in thrilling terms :

> 'Bliss was it in that dawn to be *alive*,
> But to be *young* was very heaven !'

He lived long enough, however, to find that he had been wofully mistaken, and to change his opinions ; and in later life he became a Conservative.　But this by the way.　On his arrival in Paris, where he stayed a few days, he visited many places 'of old or recent fame :'

> 'In both her clamorous Halls,
> The National Synod and the Jacobins,
> I saw the Revolutionary Power
> Toss like a ship at anchor, rocked by storms.'

He wandered about staring and listening to bands

haranguing in the streets, and gathered up a stone
from the ruins of the Bastile, which, in his infatua-
tion, he placed in his pocket, as a precious relic.   He
became a patriot, and gave his heart to the people.
He associated with the officers of the military
stationed in the city.   At Orleans he became the
intimate friend of Beaupuis, the gallant republican
general, with whom in solitude he often discoursed

> ' About the end
> Of civil government, and its wisest forms;
> Of ancient loyalty, and chartered rights,
> Custom and habit, novelty and change;
> Of self-respect, and virtue in the few
> For patrimonial honour set apart,
> And ignorance in the labouring multitude.'

Their most frequent walk was along the banks of
the beautiful Loire

> ' With festal mirth
> Resounding at all hours, and innocent yet
> Of civil slaughter, ...
> Or in wide forests of continuous shade,
> Lofty and over-arched, with open space
> Beneath the trees, clear footing many a mile—
> A solemn region.'

He pays a noble, glowing tribute to the memory
of this brave officer, philosopher, and patriot, who

> ' Perished fighting, in supreme command,
> Upon the borders of the unhappy Loire
> For liberty, against deluded men,
> His fellow country-men.'

From Orleans he proceeded in the spring to Blois.
Longfellow charmingly describes this region, which,

he says, 'is justly called the garden of France. From Orleans to Blois, the whole valley of the Loire is one continued vineyard. The bright green foliage of the vine spreads, like the undulations of the sea, over all the landscape, with here and there a silver flash of the river, a sequestered hamlet, or the towers of an old château, to enliven and variegate the scene.'

On his return to Paris in the autumn,

> ' From his throne
> The King had fallen, and that invading host—
> Presumptuous cloud, on whose black front was written
> The tender mercies of the dismal wind
> That bore it—on the plains of Liberty
> Had burst innocuous.'

France had been declared a Republic. The nobility and all titles of distinction had been swept away as by a flood, and all were alike commoners. Manifestations of rejoicing were on every hand; the air echoed and re-echoed with the roll of drums and volleys of musketry; whilst multitudes paraded the streets to the inspiring strains of the 'Marseillaise.' Cheered with hope, he

> ' Ranged, with ardour heretofore unfelt,
> The spacious city, and in progress passed
> The prison where the unhappy Monarch lay,
> Associate with his children and his wife
> In bondage; and the palace, lately stormed
> With roar of cannon by a furious host.
> I crossed the square (an empty area then !)
> Of the Carrousel, where so late had lain
> The dead, upon the dying heaped.'

The ever memorable massacres of September had
taken place in his absence, deluging the streets and
squares of the city with blood; the monarchy, as
we have seen, had been abolished; and Robespierre
had arisen, and was himself soon to come under the
power of the guillotine. That night Wordsworth
repaired to his high and lonely room, where his
feelings so wrought upon him, as he 'thought of
those September massacres,' that he seemed

> ' To hear a voice that cried,
> To the whole city, " Sleep no more !" '

The recollection of this awful period haunted his
memory for years afterwards.

Early the next morning, he heard Robespierre
denounced for his crimes, and saw Louvet accuse
him openly in the Tribune. The downfall of the
Incorruptible was drawing near. What followed in
1793, the year after Wordsworth's departure from
France, is well known to every reader of history.
The King, ' whose fate will be commiserated, whose
memory revered, whose murderers execrated, so long
as justice and mercy shall prevail upon the earth,'
after a term of ignominious imprisonment, was tried,
condemned, and executed, whereupon England declared war against France; the Giroudists fell
victims to the seditionary power they themselves
had created, and the Reign of Terror set in with
all its diabolical fury and tyranny; the Queen and

the Duke of Orleans were beheaded; frightful exe-
cutions and massacres—the most revolting ever
known in the history of the world—were perpe-
trated—seventy and eighty persons being guillotined
daily; Notre Dame was converted into a Temple of
Reason (so called); religion was universally abandoned, and Deism was everywhere in the ascendant;
the churches were closed; the observance of the
Sabbath was abolished; Lyons was in insurrection,
and soon fell; infernal atrocities were committed at
Nantes, and the Loire for a distance of sixty miles,
for weeks together, was crimsoned with human
blood. Here, as many as 15,000 perished in a
single month by the hand of the executioner; and
it is estimated that the total number of victims in
this place alone during the Reign of Terror must have
exceeded 30,000. At Toulon, upwards of 14,000
were cut off between the guillotine, the fusillades,
and drowning; whilst many military engagements
took place throughout the country. These are
amongst the events that occurred in 1793, the year
preceding the fall of Robespierre and his faction,
which brought the Reign of Terror to a close.

What the consequences, therefore, might have
been had Wordsworth remained but a little longer
in Paris, God only knows; it is more than probable
that he would have shared the fate of the Brissotins,
with whom he was intimately associated, and thus
have added another to the myriads of those who-

in that sanguinary era, lost their heads by the guillotine ! Circumstances, however, necessitated his return to England—the funds were stopped—and he reached London immediately before the close of 1792. The following are his own words on this absorbing point :

'Dragged by a chain of harsh necessity,
So seemed it,—now I thankfully acknowledge,
Forced by the gracious providence of Heaven,—
To England I returned, else (though assured
That I both was and must be of small weight,
No better than a landsman on the deck
Of a ship struggling with a hideous storm)
Doubtless, I should have there made common cause
With some who perished ; haply perished too,
A poor mistaken and bewildered offering,—
Should to the breast of Nature have gone back,
With all my resolutions, all my hopes,
A poet only to myself, to men
Useless.'

We have often thought what a divine blessing it was that he was twice preserved on occasions of most imminent peril ; first, in childhood, when he was about to perish, like Chatterton, 'the marvellous boy,' by his own hand ; and, secondly, whilst in Paris, during the Revolution. What English poetry would have been without Wordsworth, it is almost impossible to conceive, more especially when we take into account the wide-spread influence he has had, and still exercises, on the poets of the nineteenth century.

In a letter dated December 22, 1792, Dorothy,

his sister, writes : 'William is in London ; he writes to me regularly, and is a most affectionate brother.'

On his return to London, which he made his headquarters, some of his relations were very desirous that he should enter the Church, and it is not improbable that he would have complied with their wishes, but for certain obstacles that stood in the way. He had not yet been able to abandon his political theories, which stuck to him in spite of all that he had seen and heard. His mind was greatly unsettled ; he had seen his ardent expectations with regard to the Revolution frustrated ; he had lost faith in the virtue of the people, from whom he had looked for better things ; he had found that anarchy was not government ; that liberty had degenerated into license ; and he was almost in a state of despair. In a pamphlet which he wrote about this time, entitled 'A Letter to the Bishop of Llandaff on the Political Principles contained in an Appendix to one of his Lordship's recent Sermons,' the sentiments he expresses are clearly republican. He is opposed to hereditary monarchy and nobility, and believes that all titles of distinction and merit should be conferred only by the elective voice of the people. And, writing to his friend Mathews, he says : '. . . I am not among the admirers of the British constitution. I conceive that a more excellent system of civil policy might be established among us; yet in my ardour to attain the goal, I do not forget the nature of the ground where the race is to be run. The destruction of those insti tutions which I condemn, appears to me to be hastening on too rapidly. *I recoil from the very idea of a revolution.* I am a determined enemy to every species of violence. I see no connection, but what the obstinacy of pride and ignorance render necessary, between justice and the sword,—between reason and bonds. I deplore the miserable con- dition of the French, and think that *we* can only be guarded from the same scourge by the undaunted efforts of good men. . . . I severely condemn all inflammatory addresses to the passions of men. I know that the multitude walk in darkness. I would put into each man's hands a lantern, to guide him; and not have him to set out upon his journey depending for illumination on abortive flashes of lightning, or the coruscations of transitory meteors.'

Holding such opinions as these, he could not conscientiously take holy orders, and he was op- posed to the bar. Yet he had been 'sent to college with a view to the profession of the Church or Law.' His disinclination to both naturally caused his relations much annoyance, and he was regarded by them with coldness.

In 1793, in consequence of the atrocious execution of the King, England declared war against France.

This was a further trial to his feelings, and soured and corrupted his sentiments.

In the course of the year, he published his first volumes of verse, entitled ' An Evening Walk ' and 'Descriptive Sketches—taken during a pedestrian tour among the Alps ;' the former being ' addressed to a young lady '—his sister—and the latter to the Rev. Robert Jones, Fellow of St. John's College, Cambridge. Both of these poems, which were written in the rhyming couplets of Pope, fell almost stillborn from the press, attracting but little public attention. One of them, however, the ' Descriptive Sketches,' had the good fortune to fall in the way of Coleridge, who had entered Cambridge the year that Wordsworth had left it ; and he did not hesitate to assert, concerning the publication, that ' seldom, if ever, was the emergence of an original poetical genius above the literary horizon more evidently announced.' Thus was laid the foundation of a friendship between these two afterwards illustrious men, only to be terminated by the death of Coleridge. The following extract from the *Critical Review* of July, 1793, which shows that Coleridge was not altogether alone in his opinion, will, doubtless, prove interesting to the reader :

' Local description is seldom without a degree of obscurity, which is here increased by a harshness both in the construction and the versification ; but we are compensated by that merit which a poetical

taste most values—new and picturesque imagery.
There are many touches of this kind which would
not disgrace our best descriptive poets.'

Speaking of the lines or passages in these poems,
De Quincey says: 'Some are delicately, some
forcibly picturesque; and the selection of circumstances is occasionally very original and felicitous.'
Notwithstanding the measure of praise accorded to
these early volumes, they never reached a second
edition; indeed, it was long before the first were
exhausted.

Towards the close of the summer, Wordsworth
paid a visit of a month's duration to the Isle of
Wight, where a young friend—since immortalized
in his verse—Raisley Calvert, son of the steward to
the Duke of Norfolk, was suffering from consumption. Here he was in view of the British Fleet,
which was preparing off Portsmouth for war with
France. After leaving the Isle of Wight, he wandered on foot for two days over Salisbury Plain,
where he commenced his poem of that name. He
then made his way along the Wye to North Wales.
The impressions produced upon his mind by this
excursion are exquisitely portrayed in his inimitable
poem ' Lines, composed a few miles above Tintern
Abbey, on revisiting the banks of the Wye, during
a tour, July 13, 1798.'

By this time he was of age for ordination, having
entered upon his twenty-fourth year, but he was

still opposed to the idea of clerical life. Having no fixed abode, he spent his time in visiting his various friends, and in a letter written in February, 1794, from Halifax, to Mathews, he says : 'My sister is under the same roof with me; indeed, it was to see her that I came into this country. I have been doing nothing, and still continue to do nothing. What is to become of me, I know not.' Having expressed his determination not to take orders, he continues : 'As for the law, I have neither strength of mind, purse, or constitution, to engage in that pursuit.' What was indeed to become of him! He was now reduced almost to the necessity of taking pupils.

From Halifax he proceeded, accompanied by his sister, to Kendal, by way of Whitehaven. 'I walked,' says his sister, 'with my brother at my side, from Kendal to Grasmere, eighteen miles, and afterwards from Grasmere to Keswick, fifteen miles, through the most delightful country that was ever seen. We are now at a farmhouse, about half a mile from Keswick. When I came, I intended to stay only a few days; but the country is so delightful, and, above all, I have so full an enjoyment of my brother's company, that I have determined to stay a few weeks longer.'

At a loss for something to do, Wordsworth now contemplated the idea of starting a monthly miscellany, to be called the *Philanthropist*, which in politics was to be republican, but not revolutionary. In a letter to Mathews, to whom he proposed the scheme, he says : 'He would communicate critical remarks on poetry, the arts of painting, gardening, etc., besides essays on morals and politics.' But it came to nothing. Meanwhile, he was engaged in correcting and extending the poems already published. 'They have been treated with unmerited contempt,' he writes, ' by some of the periodicals, and others have spoken in higher terms of them than they deserve.'

Shortly after this, news reached England of the fall of Robespierre—intelligence that filled the poet with joy and thankfulness. He was crossing the sands of Ulverston when he heard the tidings, and he thus alludes to his feelings :

> ' Great was my transport, deep my gratitude
> To everlasting Justice, by this fiat
> Made manifest. " Come now, ye golden times,"
> Said I, forth-pouring on those open sands
> A hymn of triumph : "as the morning comes
> From out the bosom of the night, come ye :
> Thus far our trust is verified ; behold !
> They who with clumsy desperation brought
> A river of blood, and preached that nothing else
> Could cleanse the Augean stable, by the might
> Of their own helper have been swept away;
> Their madness stands declared and visible ;
> Elsewhere will safety now be sought, and earth
> March firmly towards righteousness and peace." '

He was now in a condition of financial embarrassment. His friends had been disappointed in him, and he was out of favour with them. He now, in his extremity, sought employment on the

Metropolitan press; but he was providentially saved in the hour of need. The days of Raisley Calvert were numbered, and the distressed poet nursed him with unremitting assiduity and affection. 'My friend has every symptom of a confirmed consumption,' writes Wordsworth; 'and I cannot think of quitting him in his present debilitated state.' And, in a later letter, he says: 'I have been here (Penrith) for some time. I am still much engaged with my sick friend; and sorry am I to add that he worsens daily . . . he is barely alive. . . .' Death at length arrived; and it was found that the departed youth had left him a legacy of £900.

Alluding to this most opportune gift, Words worth thus beautifully says:

      'A youth—(he bore
The name of Calvert—it shall live, if words
Of mine can give it life,) in firm belief
That by endowments not from me withheld
Good might be furthered—in his last decay
By a bequest sufficient for my needs
Enabled me to pause for choice, and walk
At large and unrestrained, nor damped too soon
By mortal cares. Himself no poet, yet
Far less a common follower of the world,
He deemed that my pursuits and labours lay
Apart from all that leads to wealth, or even
A necessary maintenance insures,
Without some hazard to the finer sense ;
He cleared a passage for me, and the stream
Flowed in the bent of nature.'

He has also enshrined his memory in a striking sonnet, to which the reader is referred.

The death of Raisley Calvert was unquestionably the turning-point in Wordsworth's career, and it is pleasing to know that his name will assuredly go down to posterity as the benefactor of the greatest poet of the century. At this time Wordsworth's religious views were greatly unsettled, and it is impossible to say what phase they might have assumed, had he not now been restored to the companionship and ennobling influence of his 'sole sister,' significantly named Dorothy—*gift of God.*

> 'Then it was—
> Thanks to the bounteous Giver of all good !—
> That the beloved sister in whose sight
> Those days were passed, now speaking in a voice
> Of sudden admonition—like a brook
> That did but *cross* a lonely road, and now
> Is seen, heard, felt, and caught at every turn,
> Companion never lost through many a league—
> Maintained for me a saving intercourse
> With my true self . . . .
> She whispered still that brightness would return,
> She, in the midst of all, preserved me still
> A poet, made me seek beneath that name,
> And that alone, my office upon earth.'

CHAPTER III.

'An elegant sufficiency, content,
Retirement, rural quiet, friendship, books,
Ease and alternate labour, useful life,
Progressive virtue, and approving Heaven!'
—*Thomson.*

Wordsworth settles with his sister at Racedown Lodge, near Crewkerne, Dorsetshire (1795)—Devotes himself assiduously to poetry—His style of living—Is visited by Coleridge (June, 1797)—Descriptions of Coleridge—Coleridge's impressions of Wordsworth, and his description of Dorothy Wordsworth—Her influence on Wordsworth—Removes to Alfoxden (July, 1797)—Composes the 'Lyrical Ballads'—Makes a tour in Devonshire—Origin of 'The Ancient Mariner'—Completes his tragedy of 'The Borderers,' which is rejected—Coleridge's account of the origin of the 'Lyrical Ballads'—Wordsworth becomes acquainted with Charles and Mary Lamb, and Hazlitt—Description of Wordsworth by the latter.

BEING relieved from his pecuniary difficulties by the timely benevolence of Raisley Calvert, Wordsworth was now in a position to settle down somewhere; and, accordingly, in the autumn of 1795, he took up his abode with his sister at Racedown Lodge, near Crewkerne, in Dorsetshire. Henceforth she was to be his constant companion and guardian angel through a long course of years.

3

Some idea of the quiet and seclusion of this, their first home, may be inferred from the fact that they had little or no society, and but one post a week. Yet, blest with each other's affectionate and helpful company, they were intensely happy, and wanted for nothing. 'The country,' writes his sister, 'is delightful ; we have charming walks, a good garden, a pleasant house.'

Wordsworth never possessed many books, but the shelves of his new dwelling were pretty well stocked, and he and his sister were most industrious readers. Their time was happily spent in reading, writing, gardening, and walking. Wordsworth was busily enough occupied. He was engaged in composing some Imitations of Juvenal, and finishing 'Salisbury Plain, or Guilt and Sorrow.' Here, too, he commenced his first and only tragedy, 'The Borderers.'

From this time forth he dedicated himself ' with all his heart, with all his mind, with all his soul, and with all his strength,' to the service of poetry. It was the principal business of his life. He composed verses upon anything and everything, sticking unswervingly to his purpose, like a limpet to a rock. No lover ever wooed his mistress with greater fervour and pertinacity than he did the Muse ; no painter nor sculptor ever devoted himself more assiduously to his art ; to excel in poetry was to him, in a very deep sense, the one thing needful. Everything was subordinated to this. Knowing the incalculable influence of inspiring natural scenery and surroundings, he invariably through life resided in the most beautiful and picturesque regions. His method of composition was peculiar. He composed, for the most part, in the open air, and his productions were afterwards committed to paper. Indeed, nine-tenths of his verses were produced in this way.

Wordsworth's style of living at this period was necessarily frugal. It was a bold proceeding on his part to turn his back upon the world, forsaking all ideas of professional life, and of employment of every kind, and to fix his residence in a secluded, out-of-the-way district, with only £900 at his command. But he was justified in so doing. Though but twenty-five years of age, yet he knew what manner of man he was, and he was fully conscious of his own strength. Having once put his hand to the plough, he was not the one to look back. He had a purpose; and he had, too, an inflexible will. He had, doubtless, counted the cost before throwing the die, and he was prepared for a life, if need be, of 'plain living and high thinking.' Such was the daily round of the youthful poet and his sister. But if their means were small, their wants were few; and comfortably domiciled amidst the beauties of nature, they had all that they required.

In June, 1797, a most important event occurred. They were visited at Racedown by no less a personage than Samuel Taylor Coleridge, destined to become so famous in the world of letters.

Let us pause for a moment to look at Coleridge. Born in October, 1772, he was but in his twenty-fifth year; but young as he was, he had had strange and exceptional experiences. He had already, in a fit of despondency, enlisted as a private and been bought out of the ranks; had been an ardent advocate of Pantisocracy with Southey and others; had posed as an arrant republican, having been deeply infected with the revolutionary movement in France; and had—*mirabile dictu*—figured as a Unitarian preacher, his first sermon having been delivered to a congregation of some seventeen persons.

He was no ordinary visitor, therefore. He is thus described by Dorothy Wordsworth, in an epistle to a friend: 'You had a great loss in not seeing Coleridge. He is a wonderful man. His conversation teems with soul, mind, and spirit. . . . At first I thought him very plain, that is, for about three minutes : he is pale, thin, has a wide mouth, thick lips, and not very good teeth, longish, loose-growing, half-curling, rough black hair. But, if you hear him speak for five minutes you think no more of them. His eye is large and full, and not very dark, but grey, such an eye as would receive from a heavy soul the dullest expression; but it speaks every emotion of his animated mind : it has

more of "the poet's eye in a fine frenzy rolling " than
I ever witnessed.   He has fine dark eyebrows, and
an overhanging forehead.'

The following is Wordsworth's description of this
remarkable character :

> ' A noticeable man with large grey eyes,
> And a pale face that seemed undoubtedly
> As if a blooming face it ought to be ;
> Heavy his low-hung lip did oft appear,
> Depressed by weight of musing phantasy ;
> Profound his forehead was, though not severe.'

And he elsewhere alludes to him as

> ' The rapt one of the godlike forehead,
> The heaven-eyed creature.'

Notwithstanding the fact that there is grave
difficulty in connection with the identification of
the portraits given us by Wordsworth in the poem
whence the first of the above poetical quotations
is taken—' Stanzas written in my Pocket-copy of
Thomson's "Castle of Indolence "'—in which he
refers, as all the world has thought, to Coleridge,
thus :

> ' Ah ! piteous sight it was to see this man
> When he came came back to us, a withered flower,'

and so on, the verses having been written in 1802,
whereas Coleridge did not return in shattered health
from Malta until 1806, we cannot admit the
applicability of the lines to any but Coleridge.   Is
it not probable that Wordsworth altered the stanzas
after Coleridge's return, prior to their publication in

1815 ? Mr. Hall Caine, in his masterly and delightful monograph of Coleridge, effectually disposes, in
our opinion, of Professor Dowden's theory that the
description refers to William Calvert, the colour of
whose eyes places the matter beyond dispute.
Besides, it tallies to a nicety with Dorothy Wordsworth's account of Coleridge's appearance.

Hazlitt's description of him is well known. 'His
complexion,' he says, 'was clear, and even bright,

"As are the children of yon azure sheen;"

his forehead was broad and high, as if built of ivory,
with large projecting eyebrows, and his eyes rolling
beneath them, like a sea, with darkened lustre.

" A certain tender bloom his face o'erspread;"

a purple tinge, as we see it in the pale, thoughtful
complexions of the Spanish portrait-painters Murillo
and Velasquez. His mouth was rather open, his
chin good-humoured and round, and his nose
small.'

'The first thing,' writes Dorothy Wordsworth,
'that was read after he came was William's new
poem, " Ruined Cottage," with which he was much
delighted ; and after tea he repeated to us two acts
and a half of his tragedy, "Osorio." The next
morning, William read his tragedy, "The Borderers."'

Coleridge was greatly pleased with his visit, and
wrote in warm strains of his friend Wordsworth,

asserting that he felt 'a little man by his side.'
And, in the following year, 1798, he writes : 'When
I speak in the terms of admiration due to his
intellect, I fear lest those terms should keep out of
sight the amiableness of his manners. He has
written near twelve hundred lines of blank verse,
superior, I hesitate not to aver, to anything in our
language which in any way resembles it.' This high
tribute refers to 'The Ruined Cottage,' which now
forms the first book of 'The Excursion.'

And now a word as to Dorothy Wordsworth's
appearance. We will let Coleridge speak first.
Writing in 1797, he says : 'Wordsworth and his
exquisite sister are with me. She is a woman
indeed, in mind I mean, and in heart ; for her
person is such that if you expected to see a pretty
woman, you would think her ordinary ; if you
expected to see an ordinary woman, you would
think her pretty ; but her manners are simple,
ardent, impressive. In every motion her innocent
soul out-beams so brightly, that who saw her would
say " Guilt was a thing impossible with her." Her
information various ; her life watchful in minutest
observation of Nature ; and her taste a perfect
electrometer."

It would be simply impossible to exaggerate the
irresistible influence of this beloved sister on Wordsworth. She weaned him altogether, at this time,
from politics, which, as we have seen, exercised such

a depressing and dispiriting power over him ; and led him, in more than a figurative sense, 'to fresh woods and pastures new.' A more gentle, loving, spiritual, and inspiring creature probably never existed. Wordsworth beautifully says of her :

> ' I knew a maid,
> A young enthusiast, ...
> Birds in the bower, and lambs in the green field,
> Could they have known her, would have loved ; methought
> Her very presence such a sweetness breathed,
> That flowers, and trees, and even the silent hills,
> And everything she looked on, should have had
> An intimation how she bore herself
> Towards them, and to all creatures. God delights
> In such a being ; for, her common thoughts
> Are piety, her life is gratitude.'

She led him out of himself, restored his mind to harmony and joy, brought him forth 'into the light of things,' and made him, in a large measure, what he afterwards became. No one knew this better than he did.

> ' She gave me eyes, she gave me ears ;
> And humble cares, and delicate fears ;
> A heart, the fountain of sweet tears ;
> And love, and thought, and joy.'

In July, 1797, Wordsworth and his sister removed to Alfoxden, near Nether Stowey, a charmingly-situated village at the foot of the Quantock Hills, in Somersetshire, where Coleridge then resided. ' There is everything there ' (in the neighbourhood of Stowey), writes Dorothy Wordsworth, on the 4th of July, ' sea, woods wild as fancy ever painted, brooks

clear and pebbly as in Cumberland, villages so
romantic; and William and I, in a wander by ourselves, found out a sequestered waterfall in a dell
formed by steep hills covered with full-grown
timber trees. The woods are as fine as those at
Lowther, and the country more romantic; it has the
character of the less grand parts of the neighbourhood of the lakes.' On the 14th of August, writing
from Alfoxden, she says: ' Here we are in a large
mansion, in a large park, with seventy head of deer
around us. But I must begin with the day of
leaving Racedown to pay Coleridge a visit. You
know how much we were delighted with the neighbourhood of Stowey. . . . We spent a fortnight at
Coleridge's: in the course of that time we heard
that this house was to let, applied for it, and took
it. Our principal inducement was Coleridge's society.
It was a month yesterday since we came to Alfoxden.

' The house is a large mansion, with furniture
enough for a dozen families like ours. There is a
very excellent garden, well stocked with vegetables
and fruit. The garden is at the end of the house,
and the favourite parlour, as at Racedown, looks
that way. In front is a little court, with grass plot,
gravel walk, and shrubs; the moss-roses were in
full beauty a month ago. The front of the house
is to the south, but it is screened from the sun by
a high hill which rises immediately from it. This

hill is beautiful, scattered irregularly and abundantly with trees, and topped with fern, which spreads a considerable way down it. The deer dwell here, and sheep, so that we have a living prospect. From the end of the house we have a view of the sea, over a woody meadow-country ; and exactly opposite the window where I now sit is an immense wood, whose round top from this point has exactly the appearance of a mighty dome. In some parts of this wood there is an under grove of hollies which are now very beautiful. In a glen at the bottom of the wood is the waterfall of which I spoke, a quarter of a mile from the house. We are three miles from Stowey, and not two miles from the sea. Wherever we turn we have woods, smooth downs and valleys with small brooks running down them, through green meadows, hardly ever intersected with hedgerows, but scattered over with trees. The hills that cradle these valleys are either covered with fern and bilberries, or oak woods, which are cut for charcoal. . . . Walks extend for miles over the hill-tops ; the great beauty of which is their wild simplicity : they are perfectly smooth, without rocks.

'The Tor of Glastonbury is before our eyes during more than half of our walk to Stowey ; and in the park wherever we go, keeping about fifteen yards above the house, it makes a part of our prospect.'

It is believed that this delightful mansion, which belonged to the family of the St. Aubins, was let to the Wordsworths on the condition that they should keep it in repair. Be this as it may, the inspiring influence of its lovely surroundings upon Wordsworth cannot be over-estimated. He continued to reside here for about a year, and he describes this period 'as a very pleasant and productive time of his life.' And such it unquestionably was. During his residence here he composed the whole of his contributions to the first volume of the 'Lyrical Ballads,' with the single exception of 'The Female Vagrant,' originally called 'Salisbury Plain,' where, as already intimated, the poem was commenced. And we are well assured that the life of this remarkable trio—Wordsworth, Coleridge, and Dorothy Wordsworth—at this time must indeed have been blissful in the extreme. What charming and elevating conversations, and enchanting walks, must they not have had ! Had the former been preserved, how invaluable would they be ! Here some of the most enraptured strains that have ever been uttered by humanity were composed—poems which will glide into oblivion only with that of the language in which they are written.

Wordsworth had a decided predilection for travelling, and it was during a pedestrian tour in Devonshire, with his sister and Coleridge, that 'The Ancient Mariner' was commenced. The idea was to sell it, and thus defray the expenses of the excursion. Concerning this poem Wordsworth says : 'Much the greatest part of the story was Mr. Coleridge's invention ; but certain parts I suggested ; for example, some crime was to be committed which should bring upon the Old Navigator, as Coleridge afterwards delighted to call him, the spectral persecution, as a consequence of that crime and his own wanderings. I had been reading in Shelvocke's Voyages, a day or two before, that, while doubling Cape Horn, they frequently saw albatrosses in that latitude, the largest sort of sea-fowl, some extending their wings twelve or thirteen feet. " Suppose," said I, " you represent him as having killed one of these birds on entering the South Sea, and that the tutelary spirits of these regions take upon them to avenge the crime." The incident was thought fit for the purpose, and adopted accordingly. I also suggested the navigation of the ship by the dead men, but do not recollect that I had anything more to do with the scheme of the poem. . . . We began the composition together, . . . I furnished two or three lines at the beginning of the poem, in particular—

> ' " And listen'd like a three years' child ;
> The mariner had his will." '

The manner of the two poets was, however, ' so widely different ' that Wordsworth handed over the treatment of the subject as a whole to Coleridge.

' "The Ancient Mariner," ' continues Wordsworth, ' grew and grew till it became too important for our first object, which was limited to our expectation of five pounds ; and we began to think of a volume which was to consist, as Mr. Coleridge has told the world, of poems chiefly on supernatural subjects, taken from common life, but looked at, as much as might be, through an imaginative medium. Accordingly I wrote " The Idiot Boy," " Her Eyes are Wild, etc.," and " We are Seven," " The Thorn," and some others.' This was after their return to Alfoxden.

At length, in November, 1797, Wordsworth completed his tragedy, ' The Borderers ;' and, in the same month, Dorothy Wordsworth writes : ' William's play is finished, and sent to the managers of the Covent Garden Theatre. We have not the faintest expectation that it will be accepted.' Certain alterations were suggested, and both brother and sister proceeded to London. It was fortunate that they had entertained no hopes of its acceptance ; for it was rejected. The reason is not far to seek. There was nothing of the dramatic in Wordsworth's genius, which was essentially reflective. Two or three years later he writes :

' The moving accident is not my trade ;
  To freeze the blood I have no ready arts :
'Tis my delight, alone in summer shade,
  . To pipe a simple song for *thinking* hearts.'

The drama was clearly not his forte, and it was well that he thus discovered the fact. He was only one of the many great poets who failed in dramatic composition.   Byron and Scott are notable examples. Coleridge, too, narrowly escaped failure; and Tennyson, in our own day, can scarcely be pronounced successful as a play-writer, backed as he has been by the greatest of living actors. Wordsworth, speaking of this work in 1843, the year after its publication —·it had slumbered in manuscript nearly fifty years —said : ' I never thought of the stage at the time it was written.' Its rejection, therefore, caused him no disappointment ; and, instead of decreasing his poetical efforts, he continued to compose with, if possible, greater activity. We cannot proceed further without excerpting one or two brief passages from this tragedy. The first was greatly admired by Hazlitt, and describes, in apt language, the remorse which follows a hastily-committed crime :

> ' Action is transitory—a step, a blow,
> The motion of a muscle—this way or that—
> 'Tis done, and in the after-vacancy
> We wonder at ourselves like men betrayed :
> Suffering is permanent, obscure and dark,
> And shares the nature of infinity.'

The following words are put into the mouth of a female beggar, who has a child in her arms :

> ' I've had the saddest dream that ever troubled
> The heart of living creature.—My poor babe
> Was crying, as I thought, crying for bread
> When I had none to give him ; whereupon,
> I put a slip of foxglove in his hand,
> Which pleased him so, that he was hushed at once :
> When, into one of those same spotted bells

A bee came darting, which the child with joy
Imprisoned there, and held it to his ear,
And suddenly grew black, as he would die.'

The two attached poets were now busily engaged
upon the 'Lyrical Ballads;' and, pending their
completion, we will let Coleridge state their origin.
He says: 'During the first year that Mr. Wordsworth and I were neighbours, our conversations
turned frequently on the two cardinal points of
poetry—the power of exciting the sympathy of the
reader by a faithful adherence to the truth of nature,
and the power of giving the interest of novelty by
the modifying colours of imagination. The sudden
charm which accidents of light and shade, which
moonlight or sunset, diffused over a known and
familiar landscape, appeared to represent the practi-
cability of combining both. These are the *poetry* of
nature. The thought suggested itself (to which of
us I do not recollect) that a series of poems might
be composed of two sorts. In the one, the incidents
and agents were to be, in part at least, supernatural;
and the excellence aimed at was to consist in the
interesting of the affections by the dramatic truth of
such emotions as would naturally accompany such
situations, supposing them real. And 'real,' in this
sense, they have been to every human being who,
from whatever source of delusion, has at any time
believed himself under supernatural agency. For
the second class, subjects were to be chosen from

ordinary life : the characters and incidents were to
be such as will be found in every village and its
vicinity where there is a meditative and feeling
mind to seek after them, or to notice them when
they present themselves. In this idea originated the
plan of the "Lyrical Ballads;" in which it was
agreed that my endeavours should be directed to
persons and characters supernatural, or at least
romantic ; yet so as to transfer from our inward
nature a human interest and a semblance of truth
sufficient to procure for these shadows of imagination
that willing suspension of disbelief for the moment,
which constitutes poetic faith. Mr. Wordsworth, on
the other hand, was to propose to himself, as his
object, to give the charm of novelty to things of
every day, and to excite a feeling analogous to the
supernatural, by awakening the mind's attention
from the lethargy of custom, and directing it to the
loveliness and the wonders of the world before us—
an inexhaustible treasure, but for which, in consequence of the film of familiarity and selfish solicitude,
we have eyes, yet see not, ears that hear not, and
hearts that neither feel nor understand. With this
view I wrote " The Ancient Mariner," and was preparing, among other poems, " The Dark Ladie," and
the " Christabel," in which I should have more
nearly realized my ideal than I had done in my first
attempt. But Mr. Wordsworth's industry had
proved so much more successful, and the number of

his poems so much greater, that my compositions, instead of forming a balance, appeared rather an interpolation of heterogeneous matter.'

Writing to his friend Cottle, of Bristol, on the 12th of April, 1798, Wordsworth remarks: 'You will be pleased to hear that I have gone on very rapidly adding to my stock of poetry. Do come and let me read it to you under the old trees in the park. We have little more than two months to stay in this place.'

His motto at this time, and indeed throughout almost the whole of his long life, might most appropriately have been, '*Nulla dies sine lineâ.*' Poetical composition was to him, in a measure, as necessary as his daily bread; he prayed for the one, and he laboured indefatigably at the other.

It was during their residence at Alfoxden that the Wordsworths made the acquaintance of Charles Lamb (the gentle Elia) and his sister. Lamb and Coleridge were old and attached friends, having been boys together at Christ's Hospital. Now, too, Hazlitt paid his first visit to Wordsworth. He had been spending a few weeks with Coleridge at Nether Stowey, and naturally enough he was introduced to the Wordsworths. He has given us a delightful account of the matter in his essay entitled 'My First Acquaintance with Poets,' to which the reader is specially referred. 'Wordsworth himself was from home,' he tells us, 'but his

4

sister kept house, and set before us a frugal repast ;
and we had free access to her brother's poems, the
" Lyrical Ballads," which were still in manuscript, or
in the form of " Sybilline Leaves."   I dipped into a
few of these with great satisfaction, and with the
faith of a novice.   I slept that night in an old room
with blue hangings, and covered with the round-
faced family portraits of the age of George I. and II.,
and from the wooded declivity of the adjoining park
that overlooked my window, at the dawn of day,
could

　　　　' " Hear the loud stag speak." '

After breakfast the following morning, seated in
the open air on the trunk of an old tree, Coleridge
read aloud the ballad of ' Betty Foy,' with which
Hazlitt was not very particularly impressed.   ' But
in " The Thorn," " The Mad Mother," and " The
Complaint of a Poor Indian Woman," ' he says, ' I
felt that deeper power and pathos which have been
since acknowledged,

　　　' " In spite of pride, in erring reason's spite,"

as the characteristics of this author ; and the sense
of a new style and a new spirit in poetry came over
me.   It had to me something of the effect that
arises from the turning up of the fresh soil, or of
the first welcome breath of spring :

　　　' " While yet the trembling year is unconfirmed." '

Wordsworth ' was quaintly dressed,' says Hazlitt,
(according to the *costume* of that unconstrained

period) 'in a brown fustian jacket and striped pantaloons. There was something of a roll, a lounge in his gait, not unlike his own " Peter Bell." There was a severe, worn pressure of thought about his temples, a fire in his eye (as if he saw some thing in objects more than the outward appearance), an intense, high, narrow forehead, a Roman nose, cheeks furrowed by strong purpose and feeling, and a convulsive inclination to laughter about the mouth, a good deal at variance with the solemn, stately expression of the rest of his face. . . . Haydon's head of him, introduced into the "Entrance of Christ into Jerusalem," is the most like his drooping weight of thought and expression.'

We have it on the authority of De Quincey that the Wordsworths received at Alfoxden a visit from their cousin, Mary Hutchinson, who it will be remembered was one of the poet's schoolmates at the dame's school at Penrith.

A tour made during the summer along the banks of the Wye, Wordsworth being accompanied by his sister, produced the exquisite poem known as 'Tintern Abbey,' which was indeed a marvellous inspiration, not a line of it being altered after its composition.

And now he was again about to throw the die. He had sufficient poems for a further volume. Accordingly, to be nearer the printer, he took up his abode for a while with his sister at Bristol.

CHAPTER IV.

'What shall I do to be for ever known,
And make the age to come my own?'
—*Cowley.*

The 'Lyrical Ballads' (1798)—Wordsworth, accompanied
by his sister and Coleridge, sets out for Germany (September, 1798)—Coleridge parts from them at Hamburg—
They winter at Goslar, where he produces some charming
poems—Commences 'The Prelude' on leaving Goslar
(February, 1799)—Returns to England—Resides no more
at Alfoxden—Makes a tour into Cumberland and Westmoreland—Visits Grasmere with Coleridge—Settles there
with his sister (December, 1799).

THE 'Lyrical Ballads,' with a few other poems, was
published anonymously in the autumn of 1798, by
Joseph Cottle, of Bristol, in a small 12mo. volume,
containing 210 pages. As this work has now
become a *rara avis*, and as many readers of Wordsworth are unacquainted with its contents, a list of
the poems comprised therein is subjoined. They
are as under :—

The Rime of the Ancyent Marinere.

The Foster Mother's Tale.

Lines left upon a Seat in a Yew-tree, which stands
near the Lake of Esthwaite.

The Nightingale ; a Conversational Poem.

The Female Vagrant.

Goody Blake and Harry Gill.

Lines written at a small Distance from my House, and sent by my little Boy to the Person to whom they are addressed.

Simon Lee, the old Huntsman.

Anecdote for Fathers.

We are Seven.

Lines written in early Spring.

The Thorn.

The Last of the Flock.

The Dungeon.

The Mad Mother.

The Idiot Boy.

Lines written near Richmond upon the Thames, at Evening.

Expostulation and Reply.

The Tables Turned ; an Evening Scene on the same Subject.

Old Man Travelling.

The Complaint of a Forsaken Indian Woman.

The Convict.

Lines written a few Miles above Tintern Abbey.

The edition, which consisted only of 500 copies, proved much too large, and the publisher states : ' The sale was so slow, and the severity of most of the reviews so great, that its progress to oblivion seemed to be certain. I parted with the largest

proportion of the 500, at a loss, to Mr. Arch, a
London bookseller.' How true is it that, as quaint
old Thomas Fuller observes, 'Learning hath gained
most by those books by which the printers have
lost !'

The volume was published 'as an experiment,'
and as a protest against the artificial style and
diction of the poetry of the period ; and its publication was not a moment too soon. That it was
received on all sides with howls of ridicule and
derision was but natural, as will readily be seen
upon reflection. Wordsworth, as we have learned,
was a reformer. He had commenced active life as
a republican ; had become deeply interested in the
revolutionary movement in France ; and now he
proposed a complete revolution in English literature. And he met the fate of reformers in general.
But the odium and censure heaped upon the work
had no effect whatever upon him ; he knew that a
reform in poetry, as in politics, was inevitable, and
must come sooner or later ; and he had not hesitated
to sound a timely alarm. It was not to be expected
that the public taste, which had long been treated to
the smoothest of smooth compositions, decked with
all the graces—if such they can be called—of gaudy,
meretricious, and artificial diction and polish, in
which there was little of the spirit of poetry,
though the many knew it not, would receive and
be satisfied with the homely but wholesome fare

placed before it in this little but highly important volume. It was regarded as an outrage against common-sense, and an insult to the judgment and understanding of its readers. Instead of having their taste gratified with poetry written in the hitherto refined and sentimental, namby-pamby style, treating of the lords and ladies, fops and fripperies of the period, they were treated, for the most part, to a selection of verses which had for their subjects characters drawn from humble life, such as female vagrants, old huntsmen, mad mothers, and idiot boys. Everybody's hand was raised against the book, but it did not for all that glide down the stream of oblivion. It was reserved for a better fate than that. It had been written with a noble object in view, and it was, notwithstanding its reception, to act as a lever that would ere long move the whole world of poetry. It aimed at being natural, as opposed to the artificial. The authors had endeavoured to fit ' to metrical arrangement a selection of the real language of men in a state of vivid sensation.' One by one, admirers were found, and a new public was created ; and henceforth the growth of the Wordsworthian theory was slow but sure.

Amongst the literary organs that referred to the volume were the *Critical Review* and the *Monthly Review*, the latter of which stated : ' So much genius and originality are discovered in this publication, that we wish to see another from the same hand, written on more elevated subjects and in a more cheerful disposition.'

With regard to the charge of simplicity and puerility so repeatedly preferred against some of the ' Lyrical Ballads,' a few remarks are perhaps necessary. It has been well said, that there is but one step from the sublime to the ridiculous; and there is such a thing as sublime simplicity, between which and silliness the distance is painfully slight. Little wonder, therefore, that Wordsworth, in his efforts to be natural, occasionally degenerated into excessive tameness, and even simpleness itself. It is no use blinking the truth. The fact is incontrovertible. Extremes are proverbially dangerous; and Wordsworth, it must be admitted, in some few of the ballads, such as ' The Idiot Boy,' and ' Goody Blake and Harry Gill,' carried his early poetical theory too far. There is a simplicity which is not poetry, and into this he fell more often than his better judgment should have allowed him. That such was the case in his own opinion, is abundantly proved by the alteration and sometimes removal of certain of the more notable and exceptionable passages which occurred in the original ballads. Amongst these may be mentioned the following :

' A little child, *dear brother Jem*,
That lightly draws its breath,
And feels its life in every limb,
What should it know of death ?'

The words printed in italics, it is but fair to say, were Coleridge's; but as Wordsworth adopted them, he cannot disclaim his responsibility. One of our foremost living writers and critics, however, assures us that he does not consider them in the least out of harmony with the general tenor of the beautiful poem, 'We are Seven,' in which they originally appeared. He sees no good reason for their omission. For ourselves, we prefer the stanza as it is now printed in the various editions of the poems. Again, after a description of a pond of water, we are gravely informed :

> 'I've measured it from side to side,
> 'Tis three feet long, and two feet wide.'

This is decidedly trivial, if not puerile. These are some instances—of which, alas! there are too many—in which the poet has greatly over-ridden his hobby, and which go to prove that a theory good in itself may be overdone. Poetry, or we are much mistaken, cannot be reduced to a system or fixed rules. Unlike prose, it cannot be ordered *ad libitum ;* it is something like the wind—'we cannot tell whence it cometh.'

Of the twenty-three poems contained in the 'Lyrical Ballads,' all were Wordsworth's with the exception of four; 'The Rime of the Ancyent Marinere,' 'The Nightingale,' 'The Foster Mother's Tale,' and 'The Dungeon.' It is hard to imagine that a reception so unfavourable should have been accorded to a volume which, in addition to Coleridge's exquisite contributions, gave birth to such beautiful conceptions as the 'Lines left upon a Seat in a Yew-tree,' 'We are Seven,' 'Lines written in early Spring,' 'The Thorn,' 'The Mad Mother,' 'The Complaint of a Forsaken Indian Woman,' and 'Tintern Abbey'—all indeed pearls of great price—unless the reason is to be found in the fact that the selection proclaimed with no uncertain sound that a revolution in poetry was imminent.   But

> 'The world is often sadly wrong ;
>   It censures him who most aspires,
>   And often most the one admires
> Who is a very child in song.
> 'But Time, that sets all things aright,
>   Proves what will live and what will die ;
>   In silence passes numbers by,
> And brings neglected worth to light.'

It remains to be added, on the authority of his sister, that Wordsworth received thirty guineas as his share of the copyright, which, soon after publication, the publisher having given up business, and transferred all his copyrights to Messrs. Longman and Co., of London, was valued at *nil.* It was, therefore, returned at Cottle's request, and by him very kindly presented to the authors.   It is worthy of note, also, that a considerable number of copies of the work was sold to sailors, who regarded it as a sea-book, so many of its pages being devoted to 'The Ancient Mariner.'

And now, having a small surplus of cash, Wordsworth and his sister, accompanied by Coleridge, in September, 1798, set out for Germany, their main object being the study of the language. They landed at Hamburg on the 18th of the month, and about a week later made the acquaintance of Klopstock, the celebrated author of the 'Messiah,' whom Coleridge humorously nicknamed 'Klubstick.' The conversations between Wordsworth and Klopstock, which were of a most interesting character, are to be found in 'Satyrane's Letters,' published by Coleridge in his 'Biographia Literaria,' and are well worthy of perusal.

At Hamburg, Coleridge parted from the Wordsworths, and proceeded to Ratzeburg, a distance of some thirty-five miles, whilst Wordsworth and his sister went on to Goslar, in Hanover, where they arrived on the 6th of October, at eight o'clock in the evening. Here they passed the winter of 1798-9, which was bitterly cold, and said to be the severest of the eighteenth century.

They had hoped, in addition to prosecuting their studies in German, to mix a little in the society of the place; but they were disappointed in this respect. Their acceptance of local invitations would, to some extent, have necessitated hospitality on their part, and as their means were humble, they prudently spent their time in comparative retirement. Perhaps it is fortunate for us that they did so, as the poetical genius of Wordsworth was now in its very flower.

He does not appear to have drank deeply of the
springs of German metaphysics and philosophy,
which so much infected Coleridge, and so largely
coloured the current of his thoughts afterwards.
Wordsworth's heart, though in a strange land,
yearned for the scenes he had left behind him ; and
in imagination he wandered along the banks of the
limpid rivers, and through the deep woods, of his
native country.   He writes :

> 'I travelled among unknown men,
> In lands beyond the sea ;
> Nor, England ! did I know till then
> What love I bore to thee.
>
> 'Tis past, that melancholy dream !
> Nor will I quit thy shore
> A second time ; for still I seem
> To love thee more and more.'

Here it was that he conceived many of his best
known poems.   Amongst others he composed ' Lucy
Gray,' ' Nutting,' ' Wisdom and Spirit of the
Universe,' 'Three years she grew in sun and
shower,' ' Strange fits of passion have I known,'
' She dwelt among the untrodden ways,' ' There
was a boy ; ye knew him well, ye cliffs,' and ' A
Poet's Epitaph '—sufficient in themselves to have
earned a richly-merited immortality.   He sent the
lines beginning 'There was a boy, etc.,' in manuscript to Coleridge, who writes in reply : ' They are
very beautiful, and leave an affecting impression.
That

> ' " Uncertain heaven received
> Into the bosom of the steady lake,"

I should have recognised anywhere; and had I met these lines running wild in the deserts of Arabia, I should have instantly screamed out " Wordsworth !" ' While at Ratzeburg, Coleridge produced some striking hexameters, which he forwarded to Wordsworth, and which conclude in strains which prove the strong bond of affection that existed between them :

'William, my head and my heart ! dear William and dear
    Dorothea !
You have all in each other ; but I am lonely, and want
    you !'

On quitting Goslar, on the 10th of February, 1799, Wordsworth commenced ' The Prelude,' breaking forth into impassioned, unpremeditated verse as he and his sister left their winter quarters behind them.

They returned to England in the same month, and, instead of again taking up their abode at Alfoxden, passed several months with their friends, the Hutchinsons, at Sockburn-on-Tees. About this time, Wordsworth, writing to Cottle, says : ' We are now in the county of Durham, just upon the borders of Yorkshire. We left Coleridge well at Göttingen a month ago. We have spent our time pleasantly enough in Germany, but we are right glad to find ourselves in England—for we have learnt to know its value.'

The circumstances under which they left Alfoxden are specially remarkable. Political feeling in

England ran high during the period of their residence there, and, incredible though it may seem, Wordsworth and Coleridge were actually under suspicion, being followed about in their various rambles here and there by a mysterious person, who was eventually discovered to be a spy in the pay of the Government. The fact of two individuals of no ostensible occupation, who were ever observed to be in close conversation whenever they took their walks abroad—and they were frequently to be met with in the most out-of-the-way places, looking at the sea in moonlight, and so forth—residing in the district, had, doubtless, attracted and disturbed the attention of some of the rustic numskulls; and, accordingly, representations on the subject were made to the authorities. Coleridge, in his ' Biographia Literaria,' remarks : ' I was so fortunate as to acquire, shortly after my settlement there (at Stowey), an invaluable blessing in the society and neighbourhood of one (Wordsworth) to whom I could look up with equal reverence, whether I regarded him as a poet, a philosopher, or a man. His conversation extended to almost all subjects, except physics and politics ; with the latter he never troubled himself. Yet neither my retirement nor my utter abstraction from all the disputes of the day could secure me in those jealous times from suspicion and obloquy, which did not stop at me, but extended to my excellent friend, whose perfect

innocence was even adduced as a proof of his guilt.
One of the many busy sycophauts of that day . . .
uttered the following deep remark : "As to Coleridge, there is not so much harm in *him*, for he is a
whirl-brain that talks whatever comes uppermost ;
but that ——— ; he is the dark traitor.　You never
hear him say a syllable on the subject." ' According
to Coleridge's version of the affair, they were tracked
for three weeks by a spy 'actually sent down from
the Government,' who skilfully managed to place
himself within hearing of their conversation as they
sat before a bank at the seaside, and who was forced
to admit that they 'were as good subjects, for
aught he could discover to the contrary, as any in
his Majesty's dominions.'　'At first,' says Coleridge,
'he fancied that we were aware of our danger ; for
he often heard me talk of one *Spy Nozy*, which he
was inclined to interpret of himself, and of a
remarkable feature belonging to him ; but he was
speedily convinced that it was the name of a man
who had made a book, and lived long ago.'

Cottle thus refers to this incident : ' Mr. Wordsworth had taken the Alfoxden house, near Stowey,
for one year (during the minority of the heir), and
the reason why he was refused a continuance by the
ignorant man who had the letting of it arose, as
Mr. Coleridge informed me, from a whimsical cause,
or rather a series of causes.　The wiseacres of the
village had, it seemed, made Mr. Wordsworth the

subject of their serious conversation. One said that
he had seen him wandering about by night, and
look rather strange at the moon! And then he
roamed over the hills like a partridge! Another
said he had heard him mutter, as he walked, in
some outlandish brogue that nobody could understand! Another said: "It is useless to talk,
Thomas. I think he is what people call a wise
man (a conjurer)." Another said: "You are every
one of you wrong. I know what he is. We have
all met him tramping away toward the sea. Would
any man in his senses take all that trouble to look
at a parcel of water? I think he carries on a snug
business in the smuggling line, and in these journeys
is on the look-out for some *wet* cargo!" Another,
very significantly, said: "I know that he has got a
private still in his cellar; for I once passed his
house at a little better than a hundred yards'
distance, and I could smell the spirits as plain as
an ashen faggot at Christmas!" Another said:
"However that was, he was surely a desperd
(desperate) French Jacobin; for he is so silent and
dark that nobody ever heard him say one word
about politics!" And thus these ignoramuses drove
from their village a greater ornament than will ever
again be found amongst them.'

Truer words than those contained in the last
sentence were probably never written, for, as Southey
says: 'Of such men the world scarcely produces one

in a millennium.' When will it ever see such another?

Coleridge arrived in England in July, and took up his abode with his wife and family at Nether Stowey, remaining there until the end of August. In September Wordsworth made a tour into Cumberland and Westmoreland, accompanied by his sailor brother, John, Coleridge, and Cottle of Bristol. The latter left the party at Greta Bridge; and John Wordsworth, after spending a few days with them, also quitted them. The two united poets then continued their tour together, and they were equally impressed with the bewitching scenery of the district through which they passed. Wordsworth, writing to his sister at this time, observes: 'The evening before last we walked to the upper waterfall at Rydal, and saw it through the gloom, and it was very magnificent. Coleridge was much struck with Grasmere and its neighbourhood. I have much to say to you. You will think my plan a mad one, but I have thought of building a house there by the lake-side. John would give me £40 to buy the ground. There is a small house at Grasmere empty, which, perhaps, we may take; but of this we will speak.'

After Wordsworth's return to Sockburn, where he rejoined his sister, it was decided that, instead of building, they should take the cottage referred to, which had originally been an inn. It was accord-

ingly secured, and they arrived in their new home
on the evening of the 21st of December, 1799—the
shortest day in the year—having walked the greater
part of the way, 'accomplishing as much as twenty
miles in a day, over uneven roads, frozen into rocks,
in the teeth of a keen wind and a driving snow.'

'The frosty wind, as if to make amends
For its keen breath, was aiding to our steps,
And drove us onward as two ships at sea ;
Or, like two birds, companions in mid-air,
Parted and reunited by the blast.
Stern was the face of nature : we rejoiced
In that stern countenance ; for our souls thence drew
A feeling of their strength.   The naked trees,
The icy brooks, as on we passed, appeared
To question us, " Whence come ye ?   To what end ?"'

CHAPTER V.

'Oh ! if there be an Elysium on earth,
It is this, it is this.'

Moore.

Grasmere described—Dove Cottage—'Lyrical Ballads,' in
two volumes (1800)—Wordsworth is visited by his brother
John—His great poetic period (1795-1800) referred to—Is
visited by Coleridge (August, 1800)—Life at Dove Cottage
—Visits France with his sister.

GRASMERE is unquestionably one of the sweetest
and most charmingly-situated villages in the Lake
District, or throughout the length and breadth of
the United Kingdom.

'Earth has not anything to show more fair :
Dull would he be of soul who could pass by
A sight so touching in its majesty.'

A more picturesque spot it would well-nigh be impossible to imagine, nestling as it does upon the
border of the lovely little lake that bears its name,
surrounded by the everlasting hills, with its white
scattered buildings dotting the green landscape here
and there like sheep, and its old church (dedicated
to St. Oswald) towering amid the abounding trees.
The lake, which is scarcely half a mile wide at its

5—2

broadest part, is a beautiful sheet of water, and
presents an exquisite picture, with its crystal
wavelets kissing the fertile fields ; while the magnificent mountain scenery, clothed at times in all
the colours of the rainbow, forms a bewitching
background which, like Cleopatra's person, 'beggars
all description.' As one gazes upon the tranquil
bosom of the mere, bathed in golden glory, or on the
encircling hills 'framed in the prodigality of nature,
unless he have no poetry in his soul, he must
perforce exclaim in the fulness of his heart :

> '. . . If there's peace to be found in the world,
> A heart that was humble might hope for it here.'

The poet Gray, who died in 1771, the year after
Wordsworth was born, has given us an unrivalled
word-painting of Grasmere, which he visited in
October, 1769. Of course, the scene has been
slightly disfigured during the intervening century.
He says : 'Passed by the little chapel of Wiborn
[Wythburn], out of which the Sunday congregation
were then issuing. Passed a beck [rivulet] near
Dunmailrouse [Dunmailraise], and entered Westmoreland a second time ; now begin to see Helmcrag,
distinguished from its rugged neighbours, not so
much by its height, as by the strange, broken
outline of its top, like some gigantic building
demolished, and the stones that composed it flung
across each other in wild confusion. Just beyond
it, opens one of the sweetest landscapes that art ever

attempted to imitate. The bosom of the mountains spreading here into a broad basin, discovers in the midst Grasmere water; its margin is hollowed into small bays with bold eminences, some of them rocks, some of soft turf, that half conceal and vary the figure of the little lake they command. From the shore, a low promontory pushes itself far into the water, and on it stands a white village, with the parish church rising in the midst of it; hanging inclosures, cornfields, and meadows green as an emerald with their trees, hedges, and cattle, fill up the whole space from the edge of the water. Just opposite to you is a large farmhouse, at the bottom of a steep, smooth lawn embosomed in old woods, which climb half-way up the mountain's side, and discover above them a broken line of crags, that crown the scene. Not a single red tile, no glaring gentleman's house or garden-walls, break in upon the repose of this little unsuspected paradise; but all is peace, rusticity, and happy poverty, in its neatest and most becoming attire.'

Nathaniel Hawthorne thus writes of Grasmere: This little town seems to me as pretty a place as ever I met with in my life. It is quite shut in by hills that rise up immediately around it, like a neighbourhood of kindly giants. These hills descend steeply to the verge of the level on which the village stands, and there they terminate at once, the whole site of the little town being as even as a floor. I call it a village, but it is no village at all, all the dwellings stand apart, each in its own little domain, and each, I believe, with its own little lane leading to it, independently of the rest. Many of these are old cottages, plastered white, with antique porches, and roses, and other vines, trained against them, and shrubbery growing about them, and some are covered with ivy. There are a few edifices of more pretension and of modern build, but not so striking as to put the rest out of countenance. . . . The whole looks like a real seclusion, shut out from the great world by those encircling hills, on the sides of which, whenever they are not too steep, you see the division lines of property and tokens of cultivation—taking from them their pretensions of savage majesty, but bringing them nearer to the heart of man.'

Such is Grasmere, where Wordsworth and his sister settled. The dwelling in which they resided, known as Dove Cottage, still retains its former character and appearance. It stands on the visitor's right as he passes through Town End. In Wordsworth's days it was a charming retreat ; and room must be found for the following beautiful sonnet, composed by the poet when in an admonitory mood :

'Well may'st thou halt—and gaze with brightening eye !
The lovely cottage in the guardian nook
Hath stirred thee deeply ; with its own dear brook,
Its own small pasture, almost its own sky !

But covet not the abode ;—forbear to sigh,
As many do, repining while they look ;
Intruders—who would tear from Nature's book
This precious leaf, with harsh impiety.
Think what the home must be if it were thine,
Even thine, though few thy wants !   Roof, window, door,
The very flowers are sacred to the poor,
The roses to the porch which they entwine :
Yea, all, that now enchants thee, from the day
On which it should be touched, would melt away.'

But times are altered.   The cottage is more or
less surrounded by the outbuildings of a large and
busy hotel; and the quiet and privacy which,
doubtless, rendered it so blissful an abiding-place
to the poet, are now, more especially in the visiting
season, things of the past.   To the Wordsworths it
must truly have been an earthly paradise ; and the
poet, deeply enamoured with his choice, took, according to De Quincey, a seven or eight years' lease of
it.   At that time the view from the cottage, since
gravely interrupted, was almost unsurpassed, the
building overlooking the picturesque lake of Grasmere; whilst behind the premises there was, and
still is, a small garden, in addition to an orchard,
through which 'its own dear brook' murmured
pleasantly as it rippled along, its banks in spring
being brightly decked with daffodils and primroses.
The views from the orchard are wide and varied,
and beautiful in the extreme.

Frequent allusions to the cottage and its surroundings are to be found in Wordsworth's poems,

many of which were happily composed here.   In his stanzas, ' To a Butterfly,' he sings :

> ' This plot of orchard-ground is ours ;
> My trees they are, my sister's flowers.'

And, in his exquisite poem entitled ' A Farewell,' he speaks of the

> ' Sweet garden-orchard, eminently fair,
> The loveliest spot that man hath ever found.'

De Quincey, who occupied the dwelling for twenty years after Wordsworth quitted it, describes it as ' a little white cottage, gleaming from the midst of trees, with a vast and seemingly never-ending series of ascents rising above it, to the height of more than three thousand feet.'

The cottage was furnished, it is stated, by Dorothy Wordsworth, who had been left a legacy of £100 by her deceased uncle Crackanthorpe. And now we are to suppose the immortal couple—Wordsworth and his sister—comfortably settled in their delightful home.   The feelings with which the noble-minded poet took up his residence here are portrayed in a passage of the first book of ' The Recluse,' which may be read in the ' Memoirs of Wordsworth,' by his nephew, the late Bishop of Lincoln, of blessed memory, and which thus concludes :

> ' Embrace me then, ye hills, and close me in.
> Now in the clear and open day I feel
> Your guardianship : I take it to my heart ;
> 'Tis like the solemn shelter of the night.

But I would call thee beautiful ; for mild,
And soft, and gay, and beautiful thou art,
Dear valley, having in thy face a smile,
Though peaceful, full of gladness. Thou art pleased,
Pleased with thy crags, and woody steeps, thy lake,
Its one green island, and its winding shores,
The multitude of little rocky hills,
Thy church, and cottages of mountain-stone
Clustered like stars some few, but single most,
And lurking dimly in their shy retreats,
Or glancing at each other cheerful looks,
Like separated stars with clouds between.'

Wordsworth was now busily engaged in preparing
material for a second volume of miscellaneous poems.
The first edition of the 'Lyrical Ballads' was by
this time exhausted, and in 1800, about the close
of the year, it was republished, together with a
further volume, the publication being entitled, as
before, 'Lyrical Ballads.' The second volume was
composed, for the most part, of the poems written
in Germany, and others of later date. Bad as was
the fate accorded to the first volume, that in store
for the second was even worse, the hostility against
it being most bitter and intense. This was provoked more especially by the since famous preface
prefixed to the second edition, the merits of which
have been so frequently discussed that it would be
idle to refer at any great length to it. A brief
reference, however, cannot be out of place. Writing
with regard to the first volume of the 'Lyrical
Ballads,' Wordsworth states : 'I had formed no
very inaccurate estimate of the probable effect of

those poems : I flattered myself that they who
should be pleased with them would read them with
more than common pleasure ; and, on the other
hand, I was well aware that, by those who should
dislike them, they would be read with more than
common dislike. The result has differed from my
expectation in this only, that a greater number
have been pleased than I ventured to hope I should
please.' And he continues : 'The principal object,
then, proposed in these poems was to choose incidents and situations from common life, and to relate
or describe them, throughout, as far as was possible,
in a selection of language really used by men, and,
at the same time, to throw over them a certain
colouring of imagination, whereby ordinary things
should be presented to the mind in an unusual
aspect ; and, further, and above all, to make these
incidents and situations interesting by tracing in
them, truly though not ostentatiously, the primary
laws of our nature : chiefly, as far as regards the
manner in which we associate ideas in a state of
excitement.' He contends that each of his poems
has a worthy *purpose ;* that 'all good poetry is the
spontaneous overflow of powerful feelings ;' that his
endeavour was 'to imitate, and, as far as is possible,
to adopt the very language of men ;' and that 'a
large portion of the language of every good poem
can, in no respect, differ from that of good prose.'
It is not too much to say, that no man but Words-

worth would have dared to publish such a preface.
'From this preface,' says Coleridge, 'prefixed to
poems in which it was impossible to deny the
presence of original genius, however mistaken its
direction might be deemed, arose the whole long-
continued controversy.   For from the conjunction
of perceived power with supposed heresy I explain
the inveteracy and, in some instances, I grieve to
say, the acrimonious passions, with which the controversy has been conducted by the assailants.'   The
critics were almost unanimous in their ridicule and
abuse, and, as a consequence, the sale of the volumes
was greatly retarded.   Some idea of Wordsworth's
popularity, or rather unpopularity, as a poet at this
period may be inferred from the fact that Messrs.
Longman and Co. offered only £100 for two editions
of the two volumes! Many a poet would have thrown
aside his pen for ever on such treatment, but
Wordsworth was not the man to be so extinguished ;
he knew that his poetical creed was either true or
false ; he had declared his faith

<blockquote>
'That Nature never did betray
The heart that loved her ;'
</blockquote>

and, after all, might he not be right, and his critics
wrong ?   So he kept the even tenor of his way, and
laboured on.   Ere long the Temple of Fame, in all
its resplendent glory, would break into view before
his eager vision, and at length he would be rewarded as

he well deserved to be.   He could afford to wait, but
it was hard.

As we have painted a bright picture of the poet's
settlement at Grasmere, it is, perhaps, only right to
state that, arriving as he did in December, he and
his devoted sister had an earnest of what a winter in
the Lake District is.

> 'Two months unwearied of severest storm,
> It put the temper of our minds to proof,
> And found us faithful.'

The visit of his brother John in the following
spring must have been a particularly pleasant one,
and in one of the 'Poems on the Naming of Places,'
commencing

> 'When, to the attractions of the busy world,'

an affectionate reference is made to the 'cherished
visitant.'   In May the two brothers paid a visit to
the Hutchinsons, at Gallow Hill, near Malton,
York, returning on the 7th of June.

Most of the 'Poems on the Naming of Places,'
in addition to 'The Brothers,' 'The Idle Shepherd Boys,' 'The Pet Lamb,' and 'Michael,' were
written in the course of this delightful year—a proof
that the Muse must have been very lavish of her
favours.   As in the case of Coleridge, Wordsworth's
poetical star was, perhaps, in its zenith from 1795 to
1800 inclusive, as a brief reference to his poems
composed within this period will abundantly prove.
And what a mine of gold do they constitute !   With

the exception of one or two pieces, the whole of his contributions to the first volume of the 'Lyrical Ballads' were written at this fruitful time, besides which he produced his tragedy of 'The Borderers,' 'Lucy Gray,' 'The Idle Shepherd Boys,' 'Wisdom and Spirit of the Universe,' 'The Brothers,' 'Strange fits of passion have I known,' 'She dwelt among the untrodden ways,' ''Tis said, that some have died for love,' 'The Sailor's Mother,' 'The Childless Father,' 'Michael,' most of the 'Poems on the Naming of Places,' 'A whirl-blast from behind the hill,' 'The Waterfall and the Eglantine,' 'The Oak and the Broom,' 'To a Sexton,' 'The Danish Boy,' 'Song for the Wandering Jew,' 'There was a boy,' 'A Night-piece,' 'Nutting,' 'The Simplon Pass,' 'Three years she grew in sun and shower,' 'A slumber did my spirit seal,' 'The Reverie of Poor Susan,' 'Ruth,' 'Hart-leap Well,' 'Peter Bell' (not published, however, till 1819), 'A Character,' 'Lines written in Germany, on one of the coldest days of the century,' 'A Poet's Epitaph,' 'Matthew,' 'The Two April Mornings,' 'The Fountain,' 'The Two Thieves,' 'Animal Tranquillity and Decay,' 'The Ruined Cottage,' 'The Pet Lamb,' 'The Old Cumberland Beggar,' and various other poems. 'The Prelude,' too, was commenced in 1799. It is almost inconceivable that most of the works by which Wordsworth is best known, and with which his name will be handed down to posterity, were written during this brief poetic period. That is to say, his genius was then in the very spring-tide of its glory—' the vision and the faculty divine ' were never brighter. Surely it is not too much to say, that had he never written after 1800 he would justly be regarded as one of our finest poets ; nay more, he might, perhaps, by some be esteemed more highly than he is. It is an open secret that he wrote a great deal too much, making everything that came in his way subjects for poetry. Certain it is that, with many noteworthy exceptions, such as his greatest of all philosophical poems, 'The Excursion,' the best of his sonnets, ' The Prelude,' and his imperishable ' Ode on the Intimations of Immortality from Recollections of Early Childhood,' he produced much after his thirtieth year that did not add a single leaf to his laurels. We think it important to insist on this point, which appears, strangely enough, to have been signally overlooked by previous writers. The world has been directed over and over again to Coleridge's great poetic era, that of his residence at Nether Stowey, where most of his lovely and best-known poems were written ; but, in the case of Wordsworth, the most productive period of his life has received but scanty notice in this respect. In the creations of his muse before 1801, a complete epitome of the Wordsworthian philosophy is enshrined, expanded and enlarged, no doubt, in his subsequent poems. Take away the beautiful lyrical and blank verse

compositions of Wordsworth written before the
dawn of the present century, and what would be his
position as a poet? The result would be pretty
much like the play of 'Hamlet' with the *Prince of
Denmark* omitted.

In August, 1800, Wordsworth received a visit
from his friend Coleridge, who, having quitted
London, where he had occupied lodgings for some
time, now resided at Greta Hall, near Keswick,
which is twelve miles from Grasmere.

Wordsworth's life at Dove Cottage does not present, on the whole, many features to which it is
necessary to refer; but a few extracts from the diary
of Dorothy Wordsworth kept at this time must be
quoted to show what a happy existence it was.

'*Nov.* 6 (1801).—Coleridge came.

'*Nov.* 9.—Walked with Coleridge to Keswick.

'*Nov.* 18.—William walked to Rydal. . . . The
lake of Grasmere beautiful. The church an image
of peace; he wrote some lines upon it.

'*April* 20 (1802).—W. wrote conclusion to the
"Poem to a Butterfly," 'I've watched you, etc.'
Coleridge came.

'*April* 30.—We went into the orchard after breakfast, and sat there. The lake calm, sky cloudy. W.
began poem on the "Celandine."

'*May* 1.—Sowed flower-seeds: W. helped me.
We sat in the orchard. W. wrote the "Celandine."
Planned an arbour: the sun too hot for us.

'*May* 7.—W. wrote the "Leech-Gatherer."

'*May* 21.—W. wrote two sonnets on "Buonaparte," after I had read Milton's sonnets to him.

'*May* 29.—W. wrote his Poem on going to M.H. I wrote it out.

'*June* 17.—W. added to the "Ode" he is writing.

'*June* 19.—Read Churchill's "Rosciad."

'*July* 9.—W. and I set forth to Keswick on our road to Gallow Hill (to the Hutchinsons, near Malton, York). On Monday, 11th, went to Eusemere (the Clarksons). 13th, walked to Emont Bridge, thence by Greta Bridge. The sun shone cheerfully, and a glorious ride we had over the moors ; every building bathed in golden light : we saw round us miles beyond miles, Darlington spire, etc. Thence to Thirsk ; on foot to the Hamilton Hills—Rivaux. I went down to look at the ruins : thrushes singing, cattle feeding among the ruins of the Abbey ; green hillocks about the ruins ; these hillocks scattered over with *grovelets* of wild roses, and covered with wild flowers. I could have stayed in this solemn, quiet spot till evening, without a thought of moving, but W. was waiting for me. Reached Hemsley at dusk : beautiful view of Castle from top of the hill.—Friday, walked to Kirby ; arrived at Gallow Hill at seven o'clock.

'*July* 30.—Left London between five and six o'clock of the morning, outside the Dover coach. A beautiful morning. The city, St. Paul's, with the river—a multitude of little boats, made a beautiful sight as we crossed *Westminster Bridge;* the houses not overhung by their clouds of smoke, and were spread out endlessly ; yet the sun shone so brightly, with such a pure light, that there wass omething like the purity of one of Nature's own grand spectacles.'

It was, according to the poet's biographer, on their departure from London on this memorable occasion that the charming sonnet from which we quote was written, on the roof of the Dover coach, though the poem is entitled ' Composed upon Westminster Bridge, September 3, 1802 :'

'This city now doth, like a garment, wear
The beauty of the morning ; silent, bare,
Ships, towers, domes, theatres, and temples ie
Open unto the fields, and to the sky ;
All bright and glittering in the smokeless air.
Never did sun more beautifully steep
In his first splendour, valley, rock, or hill ;
Ne'er saw I, never felt, a calm so deep !
The river glideth at his own sweet will :
Dear God ! the very houses seem asleep ;
And all that mighty heart is lying still !'

The following extracts are also from the diary referred to :

'Arrived at *Calais* at four in the morning oi July 31st.

' Delightful walks in the evenings : seeing far off in the west the coast of England, like a cloud, crested with Dover Castle, the evening star, and

6

the glory of the sky : the reflections in the water were more beautiful than the sky itself; purple waves brighter than precious stones for ever melting away upon the sands.

'On 29th Aug. left *Calais* at twelve in the morning for Dover. . . bathed, and sat on the Dover cliffs, and looked upon France : we could see the shores almost as plain as if it were but an English lake. Mounted the coach at half-past four ; arrived in London at six.—

'30th Aug. stayed in London till 22nd September : arrived at Gallow Hill on Friday, Sept. 24.'

And now preparations are being made for a highly important event in the life of Wordsworth.

'But there is matter for a second rhyme,
And we to this would add another tale.'

CHAPTER VI.

'The treasures of the deep are not so precious
As are the conceal'd comforts of a man
Locked up in woman's love.   I scent the air
Of blessings, when I come but near the house.
What a delicious breath marriage sends forth !
The violet-bed's not sweeter.'

Middleton.

Wordsworth marries (October 4, 1802)—His poetical
tributes to his wife—His children—Makes acquaintance of
De Quincey—De Quincey's description of Wordsworth—
Visits Scotland with his sister (August, 1803)—Becomes
acquainted with Scott—His friendship with Southey—Sir
George Beaumont—His brother John dies (1805)—Scott
visits Grasmere—'The Prelude' and 'The Waggoner'
finished.

ON Monday, the 4th of October, 1802, Wordsworth was married at Brompton Church, near
Scarborough, to Mary Hutchinson, with whom, it
will be remembered, he went to school as a child at
Penrith, and whom he at once brought home as
his bride to Grasmere, which they reached at six
o'clock in the evening of the 6th.   Before setting
out from Grasmere, he had written a truly beautiful
poem, entitled ' A Farewell,' in which, addressing his
home surroundings, he feelingly sings :

'We go for one to whom ye will be dear ;
　　And she will prize this bower, this Indian shed,
Our own contrivance, building without peer !
　　—A gentle maid, whose heart is lowly bred,
Whose pleasures are in wild fields gatherèd,
　　With joyousness, and with a thoughtful cheer,
Will come to you ; to you herself will wed ;
　　And love the blessed life that we lead here.
　　*　　　　*　　　　*　　　　*　　　　*
' O happy garden ! whose seclusion deep
　　Hath been so friendly to industrious hours ;
And to soft slumbers, that did gently steep
　　Our spirits, carrying with them dreams of flowers,
And wild notes warbled among leafy bowers ;
　　Two burning months let summer overleap,
And, coming back with her who will be ours,
　　Into thy bosom we again shall creep.'

It is easy to form a very definite idea of the
domestic happiness which ensued on the alli-
ance of the poet with his amiable and devoted
cousin, from the various references to her which are
to be found in his writings. He had long been
ardently attached to her, and henceforth almost
half a century of connubial felicity was to be their
portion. A beautiful tribute—to our mind the
highest ever paid to woman—was rendered by the
poet to this sterling lady, in the immortal stanzas,
written in 1804, commencing :

'She was a Phantom of delight
When first she gleamed upon my sight ;
A lovely apparition, sent
To be a moment's ornament.'

On closer relationship with her, however, he can
sing :

' I saw her upon nearer view,
A spirit, yet a woman too !
    *   *   *   *

A creature not too bright or good
For human nature's daily food ;
For transient sorrows, simple wiles,
Praise, blame, love, kisses, tears, and smiles.'

Eventually, having gauged her spiritual character as only a poet can, he exclaims :

' And now I see with eye serene
The very pulse of the machine ;
A being breathing thoughtful breath,
A traveller between life and death ;
The reason firm, the temperate will,
Endurance, foresight, strength, and skill ;
A perfect woman, nobly planned,
To warn, to comfort, and command ;
And yet a spirit still, and bright
With something of angelic light.'

Not satisfied, however, with having thus immortalized the gentle partner of his joys and sorrows, to whom he specially refers in the sixth book of 'The Prelude,' written about this period, he composed, in 1824, twenty-two years after his marriage, three other short poems, which at this stage every lover of Wordsworth should read, as they convey in the poet's own language his sentiments with regard to her. The verses are well known. During the interval, it should be remarked that, great as was the sunshine which had steeped the married life of the poet and his wife, the dark clouds had been many. They had drank deeply of the cup of sorrow, and they knew full well what it is to pass through the furnace of affliction. They had taken each other 'for better for worse, for richer for poorer, in sickness and in health, to love and to cherish ;' and nobly did they stand together. They had lost two of their children, whom they dearly loved, in early childhood, and they had learned by painful experience how hard and bitter it is to sit in the presence of the last enemy—

> ' The Shadow cloak'd from head to foot,
> Who keeps the keys of all the creeds.'

We append the opening lines of two of the poems referred to :

> ' Let other bards of angels sing,'

and

> ' Yes ! thou art fair, yet be not moved,'

and the third we give in its entirety :

> ' O dearer far than light and life are dear,
> Full oft our human foresight I deplore ;
> Trembling, through my unworthiness, with fear
> That friends, by death disjoined, may meet no more !

> ' Misgivings, hard to vanquish or control,
> Mix with the day, and cross the hour of rest ;
> While all the future, for thy purer soul,
> With " sober certainties " of love is blest.

> ' That sigh of thine, not meant for human ear,
> Tells that these words thy humbleness offend ;
> Yet bear me up—else faltering in the rear
> Of a steep march : support me to the end.

> ' Peace settles where the intellect is meek,
> And love is dutiful in thought and deed ;
> Through thee communion with that love I seek :
> The faith Heaven strengthens where *He* moulds the creed.'

He had thought of her, on first view, as 'a Phantom of delight,' as many have deemed their loved ones in relation to the beautiful; but after three years of wedded life he sings:

> ' She came, no more a Phantom to adorn
> A moment, but an inmate of the heart,
> And yet a spirit, there for me enshrined
> To penetrate the lofty and the low ;
> Even as one essence of pervading light
> Shines in the brightest of ten thousand stars,
> And the meek worm that feeds her lonely lamp
> Couched in the dewy grass.'

We have not exhausted our references yet, but our space forbids further quotation. For ourselves, we seek not further to draw aside the veil from the private life of the revered poet and his wife; those who do are referred to De Quincey's account of his visit to the Wordsworths in 1807, written evidently in a fit of the spleen, and published, in execrable taste, during the lifetime of all the parties concerned.

The advent of the poet's wife does not appear to have in any way prejudicially affected the domestic arrangements at Dove Cottage—quite the contrary; and, accordingly, we find the happy trio — a triumvirate of kindred hearts — agreeably settled, and leading a blissful life indeed by the quiet lake of Grasmere. Mrs. Wordsworth, it may be added, was not without fortune, which was subsequently largely augmented by a legacy of some thousands of pounds from a deceased uncle.

The issue of Wordsworth's marriage was as follows : John, born June 18, 1803 ; Dorothy, called Dora, born August 16, 1804 ; Thomas, born June 16, 1806 ; Catharine, born September 6, 1808 ; William, born May 12, 1810.

That Wordsworth's affection for his children was strong and deep is readily gathered from the numerous allusions to them scattered throughout his poems, to which the reader is in general referred ; but space must be found for a few lines from the ' Address to my Infant Daughter, Dora, on being reminded that she was a month old that day, September 16 :'

> 'Hast thou then survived—
> Mild offspring of infirm humanity,
> Meek infant ! . . . . . .
>   Hail to thee,
> Frail, feeble monthling !—by that name, methinks,
> Thy scanty breathing-time is portioned out
> Not idly. . . . .
>   On thy face
> Smiles are beginning, like the beams of dawn,
> To shoot and circulate ; smiles have there been seen ;
> Tranquil assurances that Heaven supports
> The feeble motions of thy life, and cheers
> Thy loneliness : or shall those smiles be called
> Feelers of love, put forth as if to explore
> This unkind world, and to prepare thy way
> Through a strait passage intricate and dim ?'

Wordsworth was in his thirty-eighth year when De Quincey first made his acquaintance ; and although the following description of his appearance more properly belongs to a later chapter, it is here

inserted for the sake of convenience. The great
prose-writer says :⌈'He was, upon the whole, not a
well-made man. His legs were pointedly condemned
by all female connoisseurs in legs ; not that they
were bad in any way which *would* force itself upon
your notice—there was no absolute deformity about
them; and undoubtedly they had been serviceable
legs, beyond the average standard of human re-
quisition ; for I calculate, upon good data, that, with
these identical legs, Wordsworth must have traversed
a distance of 175,000 to 180,000 English miles—a
mode of exertion which, to him, stood in the stead
of alcohol and all other stimulants whatsoever to the
animal spirits. . . . But, useful as they have proved
themselves, the Wordsworthian legs were certainly
not ornamental; and it was really a pity, as I
agreed with a lady in thinking, that he had not
another pair for evening dress parties—when no
boots lend their friendly aid to mask our imperfections from the eyes of female rigorists. . . . A
sculptor would certainly have disapproved of their
contour. But the worst part of Wordsworth's
person was the bust; there was a narrowness and a
droop about the shoulders which became striking,
and had an effect of meanness, when brought into
close juxtaposition with a figure of a more statuesque
build. . . . And yet Wordsworth was of a good
height (five feet ten), and not a slender man ; on the
contrary, by the side of Southey, his limbs looked

thick, almost in a disproportionate degree. But the total effect of Wordsworth's person was always worst in a state of motion. Meantime, his face—that was one which would have made amends for greater defects of figure. Many such, and finer, I have seen amongst the portraits of Titian, and, in a later period, amongst those of Vandyke, from the great era of Charles I., as also from the Court of Elizabeth and of Charles II., but none which has more impressed me in my own time. Wordsworth's forehead . . . the real living forehead, as I have been in the habit of seeing it for more than five-and-twenty years, is not remarkable for its height; but it *is*, perhaps, remarkable for its breadth and expansive development. Neither are the eyes of Wordsworth " large," as is erroneously stated somewhere in " Peter's Letters ;" on the contrary, they are (I think) rather small ; but *that* does not interfere with their effect, which at times is fine, and suitable to his intellectual character. . . . His eyes are not, under any circumstances, bright, lustrous, or piercing; but, after a long day's toil in walking, I have seen them assume an appearance the most solemn and spiritual that it is possible for the human eye to wear. The light which resides in them is at no time a superficial light ; but, under favourable accidents, it is a light which seems to come from unfathomed depths ; in fact, it is more truly entitled to be held " the light that never was on land or sea," a light radiating from some far spiritual world, than any, the most idealizing, that ever yet a painter's hand created. The nose, a little arched, and large ; which . . . has always been accounted an unequivocal expression of animal appetites organically strong. And that expressed the simple truth : Wordsworth's intellectual passions were fervent and strong; but they rested upon a basis of preternatural animal sensibility, diffused through *all* the animal passions (or appetites) ; and something of that will be found to hold of all poets who have been great by original force and power. . . . The mouth, and the whole circumjacencies of the mouth, composed the strongest feature in Wordsworth's face ; there was nothing specially to be noticed that I know of in the mere outline of the lips ; but the swell and protrusion of the parts above and around the mouth are both noticeable in themselves, and also because they remind me of a . . . portrait of Milton.' The excellence of this likeness was attested by one of the blind bard's daughters.

Speaking of this (Richardson's) portrait of Milton, De Quincey says, that it 'has the advantage of presenting, not only by far the best likeness of Wordsworth, but of Wordsworth in the prime of his powers. . . . Not one member of that (the Wordsworth) family but was as much impressed as myself with the accuracy of the likeness. All the peculiarities even were retained—a drooping appearance of the eyelids, that remarkable swell which I have noticed about the mouth, the way in which the hair lay upon the forehead. In two points only there was a deviation from the rigorous truth of Wordsworth's features—the face was a little too short and too broad, and the eyes were too large.'

In 1802 the 'Lyrical Ballads,' in two volumes, reached a further edition ; and it may here be noted that another was required in 1805.

On the 14th of August, 1803, Wordsworth and his sister set out on a visit to Scotland, proceeding by Keswick, where Coleridge joined them, and became one of the party. 'Coleridge,' according to Wordsworth, 'was at that time in bad spirits, and somewhat too much in love with his own dejection, and he departed from us, as is recorded in my sister's journal, soon after we left Loch Lomond.' Amongst other places of interest visited on this occasion were Burns's grave, Loch Lomond, the Trossachs, Rob Roy's grave, and Melrose Abbey ; and the poems composed as memorials of this notable tour abundantly prove how inspiring the scenery and associations were to the muse of Wordsworth. The beautiful compositions—'At the Grave of Burns,' 'To a Highland Girl,' 'Stepping Westward,' 'The Solitary Reaper,' 'Rob Roy's Grave,' and 'Yarrow Unvisited,' all belong to this period. The visit was a memorable one to the Wordsworths, who made the acquaintance of Sir Walter (then Mr.) Scott, 'the Wizard of the North,' who conducted them personally to Melrose Abbey, pointing out, as only he, perhaps, could, every feature of interest in connection with the beautifully-picturesque ruins. They afterwards dined with him at the inn. The two poets were mutually pleased with each other; and it is gratifying to know that a life-long friendship sprang up between them. The tour occupied exactly six weeks. Wordsworth and his sister arrived at Grasmere between eight and nine o'clock on the evening of the 25th of September, when they found 'Mary in perfect health, Joanna Hutchinson with her, and little John asleep in the clothes-basket by the fire.' Mrs. Wordsworth, who had her maternal duties to attend to, had naturally remained at home during the excursion.

It was in September, 1803, that Southey fixed his abode at Greta Hall, near Keswick, sharing with his brother-in-law, Coleridge, the larger part of the mansion, which consisted of two houses, one of which was occupied by Mr. Jackson, the landlord. As may be imagined, the three poets soon became strongly attached to one another. 'There were giants in the earth in those days,'—'would they could have stayed with us!'—and it may well be doubted whether such a brilliant constellation of poetic genius will ever again be witnessed by mortal eyes. Shortly after his return from Scotland, Wordsworth addressed a most interesting letter to Scott, in which he writes: 'I had the pleasure of seeing

Coleridge and Southey at Keswick last Sunday.
Southey, whom I never saw much of before, I
liked much : he is very pleasant in his manner, and
a man of great reading in old books, poetry,
chronicles, memoirs, etc., particularly Spanish and
Portuguese. . . . My sister and I often talk of the
happy days that we spent in your company. Such
things do not occur often in life. If we live, we
shall meet again ; that is my consolation when I
think of these things.'

It would be a grave and ungenerous omission in
any biography of Wordsworth not to refer, however
briefly, to his friendship with Sir George H. Beaumont, the painter-baronet, a lineal descendant of
the celebrated Elizabethan dramatist of that name.
It commenced in 1803, and came about in this
way. Sir George, who had been lodging with
Coleridge at Greta Hall, soon became aware of the
attachment which existed between the two poets,
and of their desire to be near each other ; and,
accordingly, to his lasting honour, he purchased
and presented to Wordsworth a beautiful estate
called Applethwaite, near Keswick, in the hope
that he might build a suitable residence upon it.
This would have been 'a consummation devoutly to
be wished,' since, in addition to Coleridge, Southey
also resided at Keswick. In a letter, dated
October the 24th, 1803, Sir George thus writes to
Wordsworth : 'I had a most ardent desire to bring

you and Coleridge together. I thought with
pleasure on the increase of enjoyment you would
receive from the beauties of nature, by being able
to communicate more frequently your sensations to
each other, and that this would be a means of
contributing to the pleasure and improvement of
the world, by stimulating you both to poetical exertions.' But Sir George's anticipations were
doomed to be frustrated. Coleridge, after his
return from Scotland, about the 1st of September,
appears to have been more or less prostrated by
illness, his complaint being rheumatism and gout,
with a complication of other disorders, and to have
been confined to his bed, except at intervals, for
about six months. Alas, poor Coleridge! He
now, for the first time in his life, resorted to the
dreadful expedient of opium-eating. In impaired
health, in April, 1804, he set out for Malta, where
he remained for above a year, having been invited
thither by his friend, John Stoddart. Wordsworth
was not slow to appreciate the kindness of his
benefactor, to whom he pays a graceful tribute in a
sonnet entitled 'At Applethwaite, near Keswick:'

'Beaumont! it was thy wish that I should rear
    A seemly cottage in this sunny dell,
    On favoured ground, thy gift, where I might dwell
In neighbourhood with one to me most dear,
That undivided we from year to year
    Might work in our high calling—a bright hope
    To which our fancies, mingling, gave free scope
Till checked by some necessities severe.'

His correspondence with Sir George at this time is particularly interesting. He had hoped that the baronet would become his neighbour at Grasmere, especially as he had purchased Loughrigg Tarn, and intended building by it; but this design also was never carried into effect. When Sir George subsequently sold the property, he very generously placed the proceeds at Wordsworth's disposal, and by this means the beautiful yew-trees that adorn the picturesque churchyard of Grasmere were planted by the poet.

In February, 1805, the shadow of a crushing sorrow settled over the little home at Grasmere, occasioned by the death of John Wordsworth, the poet's affectionate sailor brother, and commander of a large East-Indiaman, the *Earl of Abergavenny,* which sad event occurred on the 5th of the month, the vessel foundering, through the incompetency of the pilot, off the coast of Weymouth. The ship, which had 402 souls on board, together with £70,000 in specie, and a general cargo estimated at about £200,000, had only left Portsmouth, bound for India and China, when the frightful catastrophe happened. Captain Wordsworth might easily have saved his own life, and escaped with some of the crew, but, in his characteristic devotion to duty, he remained at his post, and perished like a man, almost his last words being: 'O pilot, you have ruined me!' Such was the heroic end of a truly noble man.

> 'Nothing in his life
> Became him like the leaving it ; he died,
> As one that had been studied in his death,
> To throw away the dearest thing he owed,
> As 'twere a careless trifle.'

It will be remembered that he had visited his attached brother and sister at Grasmere in 1800, since which period he had made several voyages, and this was probably to be his last. His intention was to take up his abode with his loved ones at Town End, and, by devoting a considerable part of his fortune to his brother's use, to relieve him from all anxiety with regard to pecuniary matters. But it was not to be. The fates had ordained it otherwise. The poet and his brother do not appear to have met but once since 1800, and that was in London, the briefness of the intervals between the various voyages preventing visits to Grasmere. We make no apology for quoting the following extracts from Wordsworth's letters written at this juncture. The first is from a letter to Sir George Beaumont, dated February the 11th, 1805 : 'The public papers will already have broken the shock which the sight of this letter will give you : you will have learned by them the loss of the *Earl of Abergavenny* East-Indiaman, and, along with her, of a great proportion of the crew—that of her captain, our brother, and a most beloved brother he was. This calamitous

7

news we received at two o'clock to-day, and I
write to you from a house of mourning. My poor
sister, and my wife who loved him almost as we
did (for he was one of the most amiable of men),
are in miserable affliction, which I do all in my
power to alleviate; but Heaven knows I want
consolation myself. I can say nothing higher of
my ever-dear brother, than that he was worthy of
his sister, who is now weeping beside me, and of
the friendship of Coleridge: meek, affectionate,
silently enthusiastic, loving all quiet things, and a
poet in everything but words.' And, in the post-
script, he adds: 'I shall do all in my power to
sustain my sister under her sorrow, which is, and
long will be, bitter and poignant. We did not
love him as a brother merely, but as a man of
original mind, and an honour to all about him. Oh!
dear friend, forgive me for talking thus. We have
had no tidings of Coleridge. I tremble for the
moment when he is to hear of my brother's death;
it will distress him to the heart,—and his poor body
cannot bear sorrow. He loved my brother, and he
knows how we at Grasmere loved him.' And,
in a letter written nine days later, he says: 'I
shall never forget him,—never lose sight of him:
there is a bond between us yet, the same as if he
were living, nay, far more sacred, calling upon me
to do my utmost, as he to the last did his utmost,
to live in honour and worthiness. . . . It was the

will of God that he should be taken away. . . . I trust in God that I shall not want fortitude; but my loss is great and irreparable.' In another letter, he writes: 'I never heard an oath, or even an indelicate expression or allusion, from him in my life; his modesty was equal to that of the purest woman. . . . So good must be better; so high must be destined to be higher.' And, in a further letter, he says: 'He (his brother) had, indeed, a great fear of pilots, and I have often heard him say, that no situation could be imagined more distressing than that of being at the mercy of these men. "Oh!" said he, "it is a joyful hour for us when we get rid of them." His fears, alas! were too well founded; his own ship was lost while under the management of the pilot. . . . My poor brother was standing on the hen-coop (which is placed upon the poop, and is the most commanding situation in the vessel) when she went down, and he was thence washed overboard by a large sea, which sank the ship. He was seen struggling with the waves some time afterwards, having laid hold, it is said, of a rope. He was an excellent swimmer; but what could it avail in such a sea, encumbered with his clothes, and exhausted in body, as he must have been !' And, lastly, writing to Sir George Beaumont, on the 1st of May, 1805, he says: ' I shall, however, never be at peace till, as far as in me lies, I have done justice to my departed brother's memory.'

What the loss of such a brother must have been to
one of Wordsworth's sensitive nature may well be
better imagined than described, and only those who
have experienced a like sorrow can at all realize the
overwhelming stupendousness of the shock. As
might be expected, such a crushing affliction soon
found utterance in immortal verse, three poems
being composed with reference to it, entitled
' Elegiac Stanzas, suggested by a picture of Peele
Castle, in a storm, painted by Sir George Beaumont '
(an exquisite inspiration), ' To the Daisy,' and
' Elegiac Verses, in Memory of my Brother, etc.'

> 'Six weeks beneath the moving sea
> He lay in slumber quietly ;
> 　Unforced by wind or wave
> To quit the ship for which he died,
> (All claims of duty satisfied ;)
> And there they found him at her side ;
> And bore him to the grave.'

The body was buried in the country churchyard of
Wythe, near Weymouth, and seldom has the tomb
closed over the remains of a nobler man and
brother.

A letter written by Wordsworth, dated Grasmere,
February the 20th, 1805, addressed to Sir George
Beaumont, contains some highly-important remarks
concerning his means during the preceding years.
After referring to the legacy bequeathed to him by
Raisley Calvert, he says : ' Upon the interest of the
£900, £400 being laid out in annuity, with £200 de-
ducted from the principal, and £100 a legacy to my

sister, and £100 more which the "Lyrical Ballads"
have brought me, my sister and I contrived to live
seven years, nearly eight. Lord Lonsdale then died,
and the present Lord Lowther paid to my father's
estate £8,500. Of this sum I believe £1,800
apiece will come to my sister and myself; at least,
would have come : but £3,000 was lent out to our
poor brother, I mean taken from the whole sum,
which was about £1,200 more than his share, which
£1,200 belonged to my sister and me. This £1,200
we freely lent him : whether it was insured or no, I
do not know; but I dare say it will prove to be
the case; we did not, however, stipulate for its
being insured. But you shall faithfully know all
particulars as soon as I have learned them.'

In this year, Wordsworth had the pleasure of
renewing his acquaintance with Scott, who, with
his wife, visited Grasmere; and the two poets, accompanied by Sir Humphry Davy, the philosopher,
made the ascent of Helvellyn. Wordsworth, ever
fond of rambling, had frequently ascended the
mountain alone; but never did he stand upon the
summit with feelings of such deep and lasting
delight as in the company of these two illustrious
men. Never before nor since, doubtless, has such
a trio stood on its hoary head, 'monarchs,' in
mind at least, 'of all they surveyed.'

It was a very productive year with Wordsworth.
'The Prelude,' commenced in 1799, was now

finished, and about this period he wrote 'The Waggoner,' the former of which was not published until 1850, the year of his death, whilst the latter was to slumber in manuscript till 1819, when it was dedicated to Charles Lamb, and given to the world. '"The Prelude,"' says Lady Richardson, 'was chiefly composed in a green mountain terrace, on the Easdale side of Helm Crag, known by the name of Uhder Lancrigg, a place which he (Wordsworth) used to say he knew by heart. The ladies sat at their work on the hillside, while he walked to and fro on the smooth green mountain turf, humming out his verses to himself, and then repeating them to his sympathising and ready scribes, to be noted down on the spot, and transcribed at home.'

CHAPTER VII.

'O, fear not in a world like this,
    And thou shalt know ere long—
Know how sublime a thing it is
To suffer and be strong.'

Longfellow.

'Poems in Two Volumes' (1807)—The Lake School—Wordsworth takes up his abode at Coleorton, Leicestershire—
Visits London with his wife, and returns with Scott (1807)
—Removes into Allan Bank, Grasmere (1808)—'Essay on
the Convention of Cintra' (1809)—Contributes 'Essay on
Epitaphs' to the *Friend* (1810)—Writes introduction to
'Select Views in Cumberland, Westmoreland, and Lancashire'—Resides temporarily at the Parsonage House,
Grasmere (1811) — His little daughter Catharine dies
(4th June, 1812), and his second son, Thomas (1st December, 1812).

IN 1807, Wordsworth came before the world
with 'Poems in Two Volumes.' If the reviewers
had conceived that they had crushed him by the
severity of their criticisms on the 'Lyrical Ballads,'
they were grievously mistaken. He was not to be
so driven from the field. Though the sale of the
'Lyrical Ballads' had not been by any means great,
yet there had been a considerable demand for them,
as is evidenced by the various editions through

which they had already passed. The publisher, as
we have seen, lost by the first edition, and it is
doubtful whether the returns from the subsequent
issues more than paid expenses.   Fortunately,
Wordsworth's circumstances had so far improved as
to render this a matter of little moment, and he had
continued to write, feeling assured that the clouds
would eventually roll by, and the sunshine of
prosperity burst forth in all its glory. As Longfellow says of Jean Paul Richter, ' He made literature his profession, as if he had been divinely commissioned to write. He seems to have cared for
nothing else, to have thought of nothing else, than
living quietly and making books.' That he had
not buried his talent in a napkin is self-evident
from the fact that the whole of the poems contained
in the volumes now published had been composed
since 1800, when the second series of the ' Lyrical
Ballads' appeared. And what a wealth of poetry
he had accumulated in the interval ! In addition
to a large body of minor pieces, the volumes now
printed included 'Miscellaneous Sonnets,' 'Sonnets dedicated to Liberty,' 'Poems written during
a tour in Scotland,' and 'Moods of my own Mind.'
No two such volumes have been issued from the
press this century. Surely they met with a hearty
reception. Alas ! no ; they were universally condemned almost on every hand, being attacked with
all the fierceness and asperity of criticism.   The

critics were galled to think that Wordsworth had not abandoned his poetical theories and principles, but had kept, regardless of opinion, on his own course. He had not bowed to their decision, nor to their ruling, and he had, accordingly, provoked the storm, and brought it down upon his own devoted head. His nephew has well said that the character of his critics 'for critical acumen seemed to be at stake; and they conspired to crush a reputation whose existence was a practical protest against their own literary principles and practice, and which, doubtless, appeared to them to be fraught with pernicious consequences to the dignity of English literature, and the progress of English intelligence.' The most merciless review came from Jeffrey, Wordsworth's implacable and inveterate foe, in the *Edinburgh Review* for October, 1807, in which it is announced, that 'this author is known to belong to a certain brotherhood of poets, who have haunted for some years about the Lakes of Cumberland; and is generally looked upon, we believe, as the purest model of the excellences and peculiarities of the school which they have been labouring to establish.' After going on to state that 'the "Lyrical Ballads" were unquestionably popular . . . in spite of their occasional vulgarity, affectation, and silliness,' and that 'there were times and moods, indeed, in which we were led to suspect ourselves of unjustifiable severity, and to doubt whether a sense of public duty had not carried us rather too far in reprobation of errors, that seemed to be atoned for by excellences of no vulgar description,' the reviewer adds : ' We have been greatly disappointed certainly as to the quality of the poetry ; but we doubt whether the publication has afforded so much satisfaction to any other of his readers :—it has freed us from all doubt or hesitation as to the justice of our former censures, and has brought the matter to a test, which we cannot help hoping may be convincing to the author himself.' The diction and versification of the poems are strongly reproved, and it is remarked : ' With Mr. Wordsworth and his friends, it is plain that their peculiarities of diction are things of choice, and not of accident. They write as they do upon principle and system ; and it evidently costs them much pains to keep *down* to the standard which they have proposed to themselves. . . . All the world laughs at Elegiac stanzas to a sucking-pig—a Hymn on Washing-day—Sonnets to one's grandmother—or Pindarics on gooseberry-pye ; and yet, we are afraid, it will not be quite easy to convince Mr. Wordsworth that the same ridicule must infallibly attach to most of the pathetic pieces in these volumes.' After quoting the first fourteen lines from ' The Redbreast and the Butterfly,' we are told : ' This, it must be confessed, is "silly sooth" in good earnest. The three last lines seem to be downright raving.' The stanzas

'To the Small Celandine' are characterized as 'namby-pamby.' The 'Horn of Egremont Castle,' 'without being very good, is very tolerable, and free from most of the author's habitual defects.' The 'Ode to Duty' is roughly handled, and 'Alice Fell' is dismissed with this withering remark : 'If the printing of such trash as this be not felt as an insult on the public taste, we are afraid it cannot be insulted.' The exquisite poem entitled 'Resolution and Independence,' which, with the exception of a few lines, is pure gold, is thus tossed aside : 'We defy the bitterest enemy of Mr. Wordsworth to produce anything at all parallel to this from any collection of English poetry, or even from the specimens of his friend Mr. Southey,'—words which, though uttered in jest, are yet, in a different sense, almost absolute truth. One can scarcely imagine that the immortal ode 'To the Cuckoo,' which every lover of Wordsworth should have delightedly by heart, could be pronounced 'nothing but absurdity.' Certain unfortunate lines, which the poet afterwards removed, in 'The Blind Highland Boy' are justly condemned, but no beauty or merit is discerned by the astute critic in the entire poem. The magnificent ode on the 'Intimations of Immortality,' which, if we, perhaps, except Milton's great hymn 'On the Morning of Christ's Nativity,' is, we do not hesitate to say, the finest in English, and in all literature, is declared to be, 'beyond all doubt, the most illegible and unintelligible part of the publication. We can pretend to give no analysis or explanation of it.' It was certainly beyond Jeffrey's comprehension. The reviewer—small credit to him—did not, however, fail to find some elegance in the sonnets, of which three are quoted entire : 'Once did she hold the gorgeous East in fee,' 'Milton! thou shouldst be living at this hour,' and 'I grieved for Buonaparte.' In the concluding paragraph of the review (?) the great 'self-constituted judge of poesy' writes : 'We venture to hope that there is now an end of this folly, and that, like other follies, it will be found to have cured itself by the extravagances resulting from its unbridled indulgence.'

After having carefully read the foregoing inane criticisms of Jeffrey, the reader will learn how little importance to attach to his invariable attacks on Wordsworth's later poems. The fact is that he did not possess the true critical faculty as regards poetical composition, as many of his essays, notably those on Wordsworth and Coleridge, contributed to the *Edinburgh Review*, conclusively prove.

Southey writes of these volumes : 'There are certainly some pieces there which are good for nothing, (none, however, which a bad poet could have written,) and very many which it was highly injudicious to publish. . . . The sonnets are in a grand style.' And Sir J. Mackintosh says : 'The

Sonnets on Switzerland and on Milton are sublime. Some of the others are in a style of severe simplicity sometimes bordering on the hardness and dryness of some of Milton's sonnets.'

So severe were many of the reviews at this time that the sale of the volumes was gravely impeded, no edition of them being required between 1807 and 1815.

> ' Ah ! who can tell how hard it is to climb
>   The steep where Fame's proud temple shines afar ;
> Ah ! who can tell how many a soul sublime
>   Has felt the influence of malignant star,
>   And waged with Fortune an eternal war ?'

The effect of the adverse criticism and ridicule heaped upon Wordsworth, had they been bestowed on many a less resolute poet, might have been indeed disastrous. 'Hope deferred maketh the heart sick,' and it is hard to find one's efforts crowned with failure. But poets, of all men, must be prepared for the worst. The Laureate of our own day was for years the butt of the critics, and he has lived it down ; neither Wordsworth nor he being the 'penetrable stuff' the reviewers in their hostility imagined. No one knew better than Wordsworth

> ' The long and weary flight
> Of steps that must be gained and won—
> The vast amount of labour done—
> Before is reached Fame's giddy height.'

And so he could afford to wait. It is almost a truism that men of genius are always in advance of

their age, and Wordsworth was no exception to the
general rule.   Indeed, it is evident that his writings
are still, in many respects, in advance of the times in
which we live, and probably ever will be.   How
true is it that genius

> ' Looks before and after,
> And pines for what is not !'

It has been well said, that ' after all, perhaps the
greatest lesson which the lives of literary men teach
us is told in a single word: Wait !   Every man
must patiently bide his time.   He must wait.'   And
it is almost invariably the case that men of pre-
eminent genius *can* wait.

Writing to Lady Beaumont on May the 21st, 1807,
Wordsworth says : 'At present let me confine
myself to my object, which is to make you, my
dear friend, as easy-hearted as myself with respect
to these poems.   Trouble not yourself upon their
present reception ; of what moment is that compared with what I trust is their destiny ?—to console
the afflicted ; to add sunshine to daylight, by
making the happy happier ; to teach the young and
the gracious of every age to see, to think, and feel,
and, therefore, to become more actively and securely
virtuous ; this is their office, which I trust they will
faithfully perform, long after we (that is, all that is
mortal of us) are mouldered in our graves.   I am
well aware how far it would seem to many I over-
rate my own exertions, when I speak in this way,

in direct connection with the volume I have just made public. I am not, however, afraid of such censure.' And, to Sir George Beaumont, he writes: ' Let the poet first consult his own heart, as I have done, and leave the rest to posterity,—to, I hope, an improving posterity. . . . I am condemned for the very thing for which I ought to have been praised, viz., that I have not written down to the level of superficial observers and unthinking minds. Every great poet is a teacher: I wish either to be considered as a teacher, or as nothing.' And he elsewhere remarks : ' Never forget what I believe was observed by Coleridge—that every great and original writer, in proportion as he is great or original, must himself create the taste by which he is to be relished ; he must teach the art by which he is to be seen.'

The circle of Wordsworth's admirers, hitherto small, was now considerably extending. The critics were not the public ; and, after all, it is the latter by whom the poet must be judged. He writes for the people, not for the reviewers, whose ungenerous strictures in the case of Wordsworth must for ever remain a standing satire on their own incompetence. It should never be forgotten that a poet, if anything at all, must himself be a critic of no mean order. And Wordsworth was himself, perhaps, his own severest critic.

It was about the beginning of the present century that the title of Lake Poets, Lake School, Lakers,

or Lakists, was invented by the critics, and given to
Wordsworth, Southey, and Coleridge ; and Wilson,
Lamb, and Lloyd, were also included in the category.
Though the designation was, perhaps, about as
foolish a one as could be devised, to our mind it
was pretty nearly as applicable as any other. It
originated, however, in a gross misconception, the
critics believing that at all events the three first-
named poets, who were regarded as the leading
representatives of the School, had agreed to write
in accordance with a particular poetical creed, and
on certain settled theories or principles. Never was
there a greater mistake. Still, the appellation was
probably as fitting as those of the Cockney and
Satanic Schools. The Republican School would
not have been an unhappy definition. It is true
that Wordsworth did, to a conspicuous degree, write
about lakes, and it is not unlikely that references
to them may be found in the works of the other
mentioned writers ; but what poet has not, at one
time or another, written about them ? It is supposed
by some that the nickname arose from the fact that
Wordsworth's first volume, entitled 'An Evening
Walk,' is a descriptive account of the lakes in the
north of England. Others are of opinion that the
origin of the idea is to be found in the circumstance
that the so-called Lakists, for the most part, resided
in the district referred to. But we are not careful
to pursue the question further. As long as it is

borne in mind that there is in general no greater similarity, either in thought or expression, in the compositions of the Lake Poets, than in those of the authors comprising the various other schools, the title can do no harm.

The family of the poet was now increasing, and the little cottage at Grasmere was soon found to be insufficient for the household. Accordingly, Wordsworth made his residence during the winter of 1806 at Coleorton, near Ashby-de-la-Zouch, in Leicestershire, where he occupied a house of Sir George Beaumont's. Here it was that Coleridge, who had returned from Malta in the summer of that year—'a withered flower'—when visiting the Wordsworths in the autumn, first listened to the inspiring strains of 'The Prelude,' which Wordsworth read to him. The poem, it may be stated, was inscribed or addressed to Coleridge, whose feelings with regard to it are enshrined in noble verse, in his 'Sibylline Leaves.'

> 'An orphic song indeed,
> A song divine of high and passionate thoughts,
> To their own music chaunted! O Great Bard!
> Ere yet that last strain dying awed the air,
> With stedfast eye I viewed thee in the choir
> Of ever-enduring men. . . . . .
> Ah! as I listened with a heart forlorn
> The pulses of my being beat anew.'

In connection with Coleorton, Wordsworth penned several of the beautiful 'Inscriptions' which are found in his works, some of the verses being set up

in the picturesque grounds and gardens of his friend,
Sir George Beaumont.

During the spring of 1807, Wordsworth and his
wife visited London for a month, and on their return
to Coleorton they were accompanied by Scott.

Early in the following year, having spent part of
the winter at Stockton-on-Tees with his friend John
Hutchinson, Wordsworth returned to Grasmere,
and, quitting Dove Cottage, removed to Allan
Bank, a more commodious dwelling, a mile distant
from the former abode. Here he continued to
reside for three years, which period, says his nephew
'does not appear to have been very prolific in poetry
—a circumstance which is attributed to the inconve
niences of his newly-erected home. But he was far
from idle, as is evident from the publication in 1809
of his ' Essay on the Convention of Cintra.' This is
a remarkable production, and is rarely to be met
with. It will be remembered that Wordsworth was
greatly shocked by the declaration of war by
England against France in 1793, when his views
were republican; now, however, he urges a more
vigorous prosecution of hostilities by England in
the Peninsula against the French ; and he is pained
and depressed in spirit, writes his nephew, ' because
when it was, as he believed, in the power of
England to have emancipated Spain and Portugal
from French bondage, she allowed the enemy to
escape by a retreat similar to a triumph.' Some idea
of the intense interest with which he regarded the

contest, may be gathered from his own words at this stage : 'Many times have I gone from Allan Bank in Grasmere Vale, where we were then residing, to Raise-Gap, as it is called, so late as two o'clock in the morning, to meet the carrier bringing the newspaper from Keswick.' The pamphlet, from a remunerative point of view, was a failure, and attracted but little attention. It is earnestly and powerfully expressed, however, and, in the opinion of the poet's nephew, 'if Mr. Wordsworth had never written a single verse, this essay alone would be sufficient to place him in the highest rank of English poets.' Wordsworth had now abandoned his republican faith, and had become a Conservative,— 'the constant advocate of a strong government, which should rigidly administer the institutions matured in a long course of ages, and only suffer them to be altered slowly and gradually, according to the dictates of experience.' It is worthy of remark that Wordsworth, Coleridge, and Southey outlived their early radical and revolutionary opinions ; and Wordsworth says : 'I should think that I had lived to little purpose if my notions on the subject of government had undergone no modification. My youth must, in that case, have been without enthusiasm, and my manhood endued with small capability of profiting by *reflection.*' Of course, the change in his political ideas was made the occasion of prolonged and bitter attacks upon him, inasmuch as, in those degenerate days, an author's politics had much to do with the manner in which his works were reviewed in the leading literary organs.

In February, 1810, Wordsworth contributed to the *Friend*—a literary, moral, and political weekly paper, conducted by Coleridge—an 'Essay on Epitaphs,' which he republished in the notes to his great poem, 'The Excursion.' The essay, which is very suggestive, and ably written, will well repay a careful perusal. In a further series of articles on the same subject, which was never published, owing to the collapse of the *Friend*, Wordsworth goes on to say, that '*no* epitaph ought to be written on *a bad* man; except for a warning'—a sentiment which is too frequently overlooked in our own day.

The introduction to a very important volume which appeared in the same year, entitled 'Select Views in Cumberland, Westmoreland, and Lancashire,' by the Rev. Joseph Wilkinson, was also from the pen of Wordsworth, and consists of thirty-four pages, as were also two sections of the work, in which he, the greatest authority on the subject that has ever lived, gives full directions to the tourist with regard to the best routes by which to get to the Lakes, and, having arrived there, to visit, with most advantage, the various places of interest. Wordsworth was pre-eminently fitted to write a descriptive account of this kind. He had been

born and reared in the neighbourhood of the Lakes ;
he had resided for many years at Grasmere, and was
wedded to the region, having explored, perhaps,
every nook and corner of it; and he knew every
inch of the ground. He could truly say, with
Comus :

> 'I know each lane, and every alley green,
> Dingle, or bushy dell of this wild wood,
> And every bosky bourne from side to side,
> My daily walks and ancient neighbourhood.'

His work, therefore, as far as it goes, has never
been surpassed, and it should be in the hands of
every reader. 'I do not know,' says he, 'any tract
of country in which within so narrow a compass
may be found an equal variety in the influence of
light and shadow upon the sublime or beautiful
features of the landscape.' Nothing is left un-
touched by his unrivalled pencil, dales and mountains, and lakes and rivers, being accorded the fullest
and most loving justice. Wordsworth's opposition
to the extension of railway facilities in the Lake
District, is well known. In 1844, six years before
his death, he addressed to the *Morning Post* two
vigorous letters on the projected Kendal and
Windermere Railway, and he protested against the
scheme in two characteristic sonnets of that period.
Speaking of the project of carrying a railway through
Furness Abbey, he says : 'Sacred as *that* relic of the
devotion of our ancestors deserves to be kept, there
are temples of Nature, *temples* built by the Almighty,

which have a still higher claim to be left unviolated.'
Lord Macaulay observes, that 'in the "Lyrical
Ballads" and "The Excursion" Mr. Wordsworth
appeared as the high-priest of a worship, of which
Nature was the idol.' Such was indeed his office.
How his spirit would have rejoiced at the defeat of
the recent Bill for the construction of a railway from
Windermere to Ambleside! Surely one cannot but
feel thankful, if only for his sake, for the collapse of
a measure which would haveled to the desecration of
one of the fairest spots on the face of the habitable
globe. May all such designs meet with a similar
fate! Are all the most sacred nooks in the country
to be sacrificed at the shrine of mammon? God
forbid! While yet there is time, let the nation
fix a line of demarcation, and, like Canute, say to
each invader: 'Thus far shalt thou go, and no
farther.'

In October, 1810, Coleridge quitted Keswick for
ever, leaving his wife and children with Southey.

Early in 1811, Wordsworth took up his abode
temporarily. at the Parsonage, Grasmere, in consequence of the owner of Allan Bank desiring to
occupy the house. His residence at the Parsonage
would, no doubt, have been pleasant enough, but,
as the poet beautifully sings : 'Bliss with mortal
man may not abide.' The black camel which kneels
at every man's gate was approaching, and in the
summer of 1812, on the 4th of June, to the intense

grief of his heart, his little daughter Catharine was suddenly called away. The child had not been at all strong for some time, but she had been put to bed bright and cheerful, and about midnight she was found to be seriously ill. The poor little thing was speechless, and her 'heavenly face' and frame were convulsed with agony. After a few hours suffering, the poet's 'heart's best treasure' was no more. She was buried in the lovely churchyard hard by, and on her tombstone are inscribed the comforting words : ' Suffer the little children to come unto Me, for of such is the kingdom of God.' She was only three years and nine months old. Yet her death so greatly affected De Quincey, with whom she was an especial favourite, that, strange as it may seem, he spent many nights upon her grave.

The workings of Providence are hard to understand, and Wordsworth's cup of affliction was soon to be filled to the brim. Shakespeare tells us, that

> ' When sorrows come, they come not single spies,
> But in battalions.'

It was so in Wordsworth's case. Six months after the removal of little Catharine, the black camel was again at his gate, and, on the 1st of December, his second son, Thomas, an affectionate boy of more than ordinary promise, was unexpectedly cut down, after an attack of measles, from which he was thought

to be recovering. The bereaved father, in the first
book of 'The Excursion,' says :

> 'The good die first,
> And they whose hearts are dry as summer dust
> Burn to the socket.'

Neither of these children had enjoyed the best of
health for some considerable time.   In the summer
of the preceding year, they had been taken for
change of air to the sea-side, where they derived
great benefit. But it may only have been temporary.
One can picture the little fellow going, as was his
wont, to his sister's grave in the churchyard, and
sweeping the leaves away, never thinking, it may
be, that he was so soon to follow her. He was
buried by her side, and over his remains may be read
this touching epitaph. Who but the afflicted poet
could have written it !

> 'Six months to six years added he remained
> Upon this sinful earth, by sin unstained.
> O blessed Lord ! whose mercy then removed
> A child whom every eye that looked on loved,
> Support us ! teach us calmly to resign
> What we possessed, and now is wholly Thine.'

Only those who have lost the tender buds of affection can have the faintest conception of the anguish
into which the loving Wordsworth was plunged by
these overwhelming sorrows.   The iron must have
entered into his very soul.   But as the tree strikes
deeper when its boughs are riven by the tempest, so
his confidence and trust in Providence seem to have

been strengthened by the stern discipline of adversity. Who can doubt the truth of what his brother-poet Rogers sings :

> ' The good are better made by ill,
> As odours crushed are sweeter still '?

Wordsworth, as may be imagined, could not live much longer in the Parsonage, within and without which everything reminded him of his grief, and, in a letter dated January the 8th, 1813, he writes to Lord Lonsdale : 'The house which I have for some time occupied, is the Parsonageof Grasmere. It stands close by the churchyard, and I have found it absolutely necessary that we should quit a place which, by recalling to our minds at every moment the losses we have sustained in the course of the last year, would grievously retard our progress towards that tranquillity which it is our duty to aim at.'

CHAPTER VIII.

*'This castle hath a pleasant seat ; the air
Nimbly and sweetly recommends itself
Unto our gentle senses. . . . . . .
. . . . The heaven's breath
Smells wooingly here.'*

Shakespeare.

Wordsworth removes to Rydal Mount (1813)—Description of the same—Is appointed Distributor of Stamps for Westmoreland—Declines the Collectorship of Whitehaven—'The Excursion' (1814) — 'Poems: including Lyrical Ballads, etc.,' in two volumes (1815)—'The White Doe of Rylstone' (1815)—Extracts from the poem.

ACCORDINGLY, in the spring of 1813, Wordsworth, with his family, quitted Grasmere, and removed to Rydal Mount, which had but recently become vacant, and which was to be his abode for nearly forty years. This beautiful residence—next to Shakespeare's the most celebrated from a poetical standpoint in the world — which has since become immortalized, was all that could be desired, being, with its exquisitely-picturesque surroundings, such a sight indeed

*' As youthful poets dream
On summer eves by haunted stream.'*

In the year of Wordsworth's death, his nephew thus described the dwelling : 'It is a modest mansion, of a sober hue, tinged with weather stains, with two tiers of five windows; on the right of these is a porch, and above, and to the right, are two other windows ; the highest looks out of what was the poet's bedroom. The gable end at the east, that first seen on entering the grounds from the road, presents on the ground-floor the window of the old hall or dining-room. The house is mantled over here and there with roses and ivy, and jessamine and Virginia creeper.' Such as it then was, it is in a great measure now, notwithstanding certain alterations which have been effected. Harriet Martineau describes the garden as a 'true poet's garden,' and Miss Jewsbury, in the *Literary Magnet* for 1826, has charmingly sketched 'The Poet's Home.' This is the word-painting :

> ' Low and white, yet scarcely seen
> Are its walls for mantling green ;
> Not a window lets in light
> But through flowers clustering bright :
> Not a glance may wander there
> But it falls on something fair ;
> Garden choice, and fairy mound,
> Only that no elves are found ;
> Winding walk, and sheltered nook,
> For student grave and graver book :
> Or a birdlike bower, perchance,
> Fit for maiden and romance.
> Then, far off, a glorious sheen
> Of wide and sunlit waters seen ;
> Hills that in the distance lie,
> Blue and yielding as the sky ;

And nearer, closing round the nest,
The home, of all the "living crest,"
Other rocks and mountains stand,
Rugged, yet a guardian band,
Like those that did, in fable old,
Elysium from the world enfold.'

Mrs. Hemans, in one of her delightful letters, depicts the house as 'a lovely cottage-like building, almost hidden by a profusion of roses and ivy.'

Rydal Mount, which is about a mile and a half from Grasmere, and a like distance from Ambleside, stands at an imposing elevation on the sloping side of Nab Scar, with a southern aspect, immediately above Rydal Water, with its enchanting fairy islets and bewitching shores, and commands unrivalled views of the beautiful and romantic valley of the Rothay, and of the gleaming lake of Windermere, spread far away like a sheet of silver; while in front, and on the right, rise the densely-wooded fells of Loughrigg, with Wansfell, which catches the last resplendent rays of the setting sun, on the left—the whole composing a picture such as it would never have entered into the heart of man to conceive, and which once beheld in all the glory of a summer day, or sleeping in the radiance of the moon, can never be forgotten.

The poet's family now consisted of himself, his wife, and three children, in addition to his devoted sister Dorothy, and his sister-in-law, Sarah Hutchinson, whom he loved almost as his own sister. Surely, if ever a man were blessed with the inspiring society, help, and sympathy, of exalted and ennobling women, Wordsworth was; and it cannot be denied that they contributed, in a high degree, to make him what he was. All honour to their memory.

The year of Wordsworth's removal to Rydal Mount was signalized by a remarkable stroke of good fortune, the appointment of Distributor of Stamps in the county of Westmoreland being conferred upon him on the 27th of March. This office was procured for him through the influence of his noble friend the Earl of Lonsdale, and added to his income, according to De Quincey, 'somewhere about £500 a year'—a most acceptable addition, more especially when it is remembered that its duties could be satisfactorily discharged by deputy. His coadjutor, John Carter, proved invaluable, rendering 'yeoman's service' not only in his official capacity, but also, says the poet's nephew, as 'a vigilant corrector of the press, a sound scholar, and a judicious critic.' He served the poet faithfully and most efficiently until the death of the latter in 1850, when it was found that he was nominated one of the executors under the will—an act which speaks volumes as to the high esteem in which he was held by Wordsworth.

Some time after the appointment referred to had been bestowed upon Wordsworth, he was offered a much more important and lucrative position—that of Collector of Whitehaven; but he was so endeared to the beautiful district in which he resided that he was induced to decline it; and, in so doing, it cannot be doubted that he acted wisely.

The fame of the poet at this period was largely increasing, notwithstanding the fact that his publications had but a very limited sale. The verse cast upon the literary waters was destined to float, having in it not only the elements of life, but of immortality also. Southey, in 1804, to his honour, had not hesitated to write: 'Wordsworth will do better (than Coleridge), and leave behind him a name, unique in his way; he will rank among the very first poets, and probably possesses a mass of merits superior to all, except only Shakespeare.'

In 1814, after having made a tour in Scotland accompanied by his wife and her sister, Wordsworth published his *magnum opus*, 'The Excursion,' which he dedicated in a graceful sonnet to his illustrious friend and benefactor, the Earl of Lonsdale. The edition, which is in quarto, and contains 447 pages, consisted of 500 copies. It need scarcely be stated, that the volume shared no better fate than its predecessors, the leading reviews being most hostile; and had the reviewers been the public, which fortunately was not the case, it would speedily have glided down the stream of that oblivion to which they unmercifully doomed it. Jeffrey, in the

Edinburgh Review, poured forth all the vials of his wrath, hatred, and indignation upon it, in what may well be termed the most memorable critique of the century, with which most readers of this biography are probably acquainted.   Determined to extinguish the author, the critic, in his fury, begins : 'This will never do !' and he then proceeds to hurl forth all the thunderbolts of literary criticism at his command. He even went so far afterwards as to boast that he had crushed the poem.   But the writer, in his blindness and self-assurance, grievously over-estimated even his mighty strength, and he failed to effect his malicious purpose.   The work, however, was not without supporters in more discerning quarters. Southey, one of the greatest critics of his day, writing in December, 1814, to his friend Scott, says : 'Jeffrey, I hear, has written what his admirers call a *crushing* review of " The Excursion."   He might as well seat himself upon Skiddaw and fancy that he crushed the mountain.   I heartily wish Wordsworth may one day meet with him, and lay him alongside, yard-arm and yard-arm in argument.'   Bravo, Southey!   The opinion of Southey with regard to Jeffrey finds a fitting place here.   He writes : ' To Jeffrey, as an individual, I shall ever be ready to show individual courtesy, but of Judge Jeffrey of the *Edinburgh Review,* I must ever think and speak as of a bad politician, a worse moralist, and a critic, in matters of taste, equally incompetent and unjust.'   'I have often wished,' says Coleridge, 'that the first two books of "The Excursion" had been published separately, under the name of "The Deserted Cottage." They would have formed, what indeed they are, one of the most beautiful poems in the language.' 'In power of intellect,' says Hazlitt, 'in lofty conception, in the depth of feeling, at once simple and sublime, which pervades every part of it, and which gives to every object an almost preternatural and preter-human interest, this work has seldom been surpassed.' Professor Wilson, in 'The Recreations of Christopher North,' writes : '"The Excursion" is a series of poems, all swimming in the light of poetry; some of them sweet and simple; some elegant and graceful; some beautiful and most lovely ; some of strength and state ; some majestic ; some magnificent ; some sublime.' Byron, who had severely satirized Wordsworth in his 'English Bards and Scotch Reviewers,' written in 1808, describes it as

> 'A drowsy, frowzy poem, called *The Excursion*,
> Writ it in a manner which is my aversion.'

This truly great philosophical poem, which was commenced in 1795, at Racedown, was completed at Grasmere, the greater proportion of it being written at Allan Bank. The poet's nephew would seem to have overlooked this, in remarking, that the three years' residence there did not appear to be 'very

prolific in poetry.' 'The Excursion' was published
as ' being a portion of "The Recluse,"' the author's
intention, when he retired to his native mountains,
being ' to construct a literary work that might live.'
This great undertaking was to be entitled 'The
Recluse,' and was to consist of three parts, that
charming autobiographical poem finished in 1805,
which remained in manuscript until 1850—the
year of the poet's death—when it was given to the
world under the title of 'The Prelude,' being the
first part ; 'The Excursion,' the second ; and the conclusion, which was never accomplished, the third.
The principal subject of ' The Recluse,' says Wordsworth, was to be 'the sensations and opinions of.
a poet living in retirement,' and the poem was to
contain views ' of Man, Nature, and Society.' In
'The Excursion,' Wordsworth appears in what was
unquestionably his greatest character — that of a
lofty metaphysical poet—and it is now universally
admitted that, slight as is the framework of this
noble poem, the plot being little or nothing, it
abounds with beauties of the highest poetical order ;
flights of fancy and inspired reflection that leave
nothing to be desired ; and descriptions of mountain scenery, and of human life, that have never
been eclipsed.   Yet the volume, it must be confessed, fell almost still-born from the press.   The
work is not without grave defects, the weakness of
the poet in so long and sustained an effort being

9

frequently apparent, many passages being nothing but the most prosaic of disquisitions. But its faults, it is needless to say, are infinitely more than overbalanced by its innumerable beauties and excellencies, which come upon the reader like revelations. It would be a waste of time to enumerate the most admired passages in a poem almost every page of which is a *florilegium ;* the reader will best consult his own interest by perusing the work and seeking for them. He will never begrudge the time thus spent ; on the contrary, he will rise from the perusal a richer and a better man. He will find his views with regard to his fellow-creatures extended and exalted ; his despondency, into which all are too prone to lapse, will be corrected ; he will be led into closer and more active communion with Nature ; and he will learn, as his faith is strengthened, that it is true philosophy to educe good from evil. Wordsworth is essentially a didactic poet, but his didacticism is of the most agreeable kind. And in 'The Excursion' he comes before us as a high and lofty metaphysical and philosophical teacher, and we cannot forbid the thought that, in this stupendous monument of his genius, he speaks most, as it were, in his original character—we converse with him in his wanderings, and, as we drink in the ennobling utterances which fall from his sacred lips, we are at one with him ; we feel that we know him ' in his habit as he lived;' we are drawn irresistibly towards him ; and we love him as, perhaps, we never loved him before. In a letter to Southey, in which he refers to some of the reviews of the poem, he says : 'Let the age continue to love its own darkness ; I shall continue to write with, I trust, the light of Heaven upon me.' It is discouraging to learn how Wordsworth was, for the most part, regarded by his contemporaries ; but there are parallel cases, and their name is legion, to be found, from the Christian era, to go no further back, downwards. We read of a greater than Wordsworth that ' He came unto His own, and His own received Him not.' The effect of the critiques on ' The Excursion ' proved so injurious that no further edition was required for six years ; but the poet had the deep gratification of seeing it run through several before his death.

It is a noteworthy fact that Wordsworth was singularly unfortunate in the time of publication of his greatest poem. A glance at the poets most in esteem at that period will at once show this. At least half-a-dozen were then in the very zenith of their popularity : Southey, who was poet-laureate, Byron, Scott, Rogers, Moore, and Campbell ; all of whom were poets of a very different order from Wordsworth. Amongst the celebrated poems that had been published between 1810 and 1814, inclusive, were 'The Curse of Kehama' (1810), the first and second cantos of ' Childe Harold ' (1812), 'The

Giaour,' and 'The Bride of Abydos' (1813), 'The
Lady of the Lake' (1810), 'The Vision of Don
Roderick' (1811), and 'Rokeby,' and 'The Bridal
of Triermain' (1813). With the exception of the
first-named work, which is the corner-stone of
Southey's poetical fabric, all these compositions were
well adapted to catch the public ear, being readily
understood and enjoyed without reflection. The
spirit of the age was romantic, and it was, perhaps,
too much to expect that readers who craved for exciting food of the kind referred to either would or
could relish the wholesome contemplative and
spiritual repast to which they were treated by
Wordsworth. They would not have that man to
reign over them. But, as Tennyson truly observes,
'the old order changeth, yielding place to new ;' and
the avidity with which the romances of the day
were devoured, produced an excess of imitative work
of vastly inferior quality, which speedily created a
surfeit, to which it would appear the poetry of
Wordsworth formed a powerful corrective. There
are two classes of food—that which pleases, but
does not satisfy, and that which satisfies no less than
it pleases. Wordsworth's literary fare distinctly belongs to the latter. He is peculiarly a poet *su*
generis. Delightful as are all the great poets, there
are times and moods in which the thoughtful reader
turns from them all, and in communion with Wordsworth invariably finds solace and rest. Wordsworth

is naturally the poet of meditation, and it is good and necessary occasionally to withdraw ourselves 'far from the madding crowd,' and to hold sweet converse with our own hearts.   And the man who cannot see himself in Wordsworth's poetry, must indeed be utterly destitute of 'the vision and the faculty divine.'   Alas! there are too many in this miserable condition.

In 1815, Wordsworth issued, in two volumes, ' Poems : including Lyrical Ballads, and the Miscellaneous Pieces of the Author; with Additional Poems, a New Preface, and a Supplementary Essay.' The work was gracefully inscribed to his devoted friend Sir George Beaumont, and contained a remarkably fine and masterly preface, in which, amongst other things, he explains the principles on which he then, for the first time, divided his poetical compositions into classes, such as 'Poems founded on the Affections,' 'Poems of Sentiment and Reflection,' ' Poems of the Fancy,' etc.   Writing to a friend in 1816, Southey says : ' Have you read " The Excursion ?" and have you read the collection of Wordsworth's other poems, in two octavo volumes? If you have not, there is a great pleasure in store for you. . . . It is by the side of Milton that Wordsworth will have his station awarded him by posterity.'   We shall reserve for a later chapter what few remarks we have to offer on the classification of the poems, to which we have thus briefly alluded.

Many writers on Wordsworth, strange to relate
have overlooked the publication of these highly
important volumes.

In the same year (1815), Wordsworth publishe
his poem entitled 'The White Doe of Rylstone; or
the Fate of the Nortons,' the work, which wa
tenderly dedicated to his wife in some beautifu
prefatory verses, being issued from the press in
quarto. This elegant creation is founded on a tradi
tion connected with Bolton Priory, in Yorkshire
and was the outcome of a visit which the poet pai
to the district, which abounds with enchantin
scenery, in the summer of 1807. 'The earlier hal
of this poem,' said Wordsworth, 'was composed a
Stockton-upon-Tees, when Mary and I were on
visit to her eldest brother, Mr. Hutchinson, at th
close of the year 1807.' On their return to Gra
mere, it was continued, and in all probability com
pleted there. The poem, which is narrativ
throughout, and written in irregular metre an
stanzas, is a charming composition, and contain
some exquisite descriptive passages, two of whicl
the reader will thank us for quoting. A servic
is being held in the 'rural chapel,' which forms par
of the Priory ; a hymn is sung ; after which, al
being hushed, the priest 'recites the holy liturgy :'

'When soft !—the dusky trees between,
And down the path through the open green,
Where is no living thing to be seen ;

And through yon gateway, where is found,
Beneath the arch with ivy bound,
Free entrance to the church-yard ground ;
And right across the verdant sod
Towards the very house of God ;—
Comes gliding in with lovely gleam,
  Comes gliding in serene and slow,
Soft and silent as a dream,
  A solitary doe !
White she is as lily of June,
And beauteous as the silver moon
When out of sight the clouds are driven,
And she is left alone in heaven ;
Or like a ship some gentle day
In sunshine sailing far away,
A glittering ship, that hath the plain
Of ocean for her own domain.'

If this is not the truest of true poetry, what is ?

The second passage is no less delightful.   None
but a poet of the very highest order could have
penned it.   But we must not anticipate the reader's
judgment.   Let the lines be read aloud.

' From cloudless ether looking down,
  The moon, this tranquil evening, sees
A camp and a beleaguered town,
And castle like a stately crown
  On the steep rocks of winding Tees ;
And southward far, with moors between,
Hill-tops, and floods, and forest green,
The bright moon sees that valley small
Where Rylstone's old sequestered hall
A venerable image yields
Of quiet to the neighbouring fields ;
While from one pillared chimney breathes
The smoke, and mounts in silver wreaths.
The courts are hushed ;—for timely sleep
The greyhounds to their kennel creep ;

> The peacock in a broad ash-tree
>   Aloft is roosted for the night,
> He who in proud prosperity
>   Of colours manifold and bright
>   Walked round, affronting the daylight ;
> And higher still above the bower
> Where he is perched, from yon lone tower
> The hall-clock in the clear moonshine
> With glittering finger points at nine.'

There are many superb descriptions of moon-lit scenes in English poetry, but we doubt whether a more delicately-lovely picture than this has ever been painted. The poem, from beginning to end, is instinct with the genius of the poet, and bears his sign-manual almost on its every line. Strangely enough, it contains few, if any, lines or passages which have passed into quotations. Neither was it likely to become rapidly popular. ' Of the " White Doe," ' observes Wordsworth, ' I have little to say, but that I hope it will be acceptable to the intelligent, for whom alone it is written.' And Dorothy Wordsworth writes : ' Some of our friends, who are equal admirers of the " White Doe " and of my brother's published poems, think that *this* poem will sell on account of the story ; that is, that the story will bear up those points which are above the level of the public taste ; whereas the two last volumes—except by a few solitary individuals, who are passionately devoted to my brother's works—are abused by wholesale.

' Now, as his sole object in publishing this poem

at present would be for the sake of the money, he
would not publish it if he did not think, from the
several judgments of his friends, that it would be
likely to have a sale. He has no pleasure in publishing—he even detests it; and if it were not that he
is *not* over wealthy, he would leave all his works to
be published after his death. William himself is
sure that the " White Doe " will not sell or be
admired, except by a very few, at first; and only
yields to Mary's entreaties and mine. We are
determined, however, if we are deceived this time,
to let him have his own way in future.'

Now, how was the work received ! Jeffrey, in
the *Edinburgh Review*, with his usual asperity to
Wordsworth, declares: 'This, we think, has the
merit of being the very worst poem we ever saw
imprinted in a quarto volume. . . . In the " Lyrical
Ballads " he (Wordsworth) was exhibited, on the
whole, in a vein of very pretty deliration; but in
the poem before us he appears in a state of low and
maudlin imbecility, which would not have mis-
become Master Silence himself, in the close of a
social day.' *Verbum sap.* Jeffrey was clearly not one
of ' the intelligent, for whom alone it was written.'

Wordsworth's notion of the poem was as high as
Jeffrey's was low; and it is narrated that on one
occasion he inquired of his friend Davy :

' Do you know the reason why I published
" The White Doe " in quarto ?'

'No,' replied Davy ; 'what was it ?'

'To show the world my own opinion of it,' rejoined the poet.

It may be stated, that, in conception, this poem was in Wordsworth's estimation the greatest production of his muse. The work, notwithstanding its merits, which are unquestionable, never reached a second edition during the poet's lifetime.

CHAPTER IX.

'Domestic Happiness, thou only bliss
Of Paradise that has survived the fall !'
                                        Cowper.

Wordsworth's domestic happiness—Leigh Hunt's account of
   his appearance—His literary friendships—His brother
   Richard dies (1816)—'Peter Bell' (1819)—'The Waggoner'
   (1819)—'The River Duddon,' etc. (1820)—Visits Switzerland and Italy, and, returning, narrowly escapes shipwreck
   (1820)—Is thrown from his horse and seriously injured
   (1822)—'Memorials of a tour on the Continent, 1820'
   (1822)—'Ecclesiastical Sketches' (1822)—Visits Belgium
   and Holland (1823)—Makes a tour in North Wales (1824)
   —His library—His habit of reading and correcting his own
   poems—Sir George Beaumont dies, and leaves him an
   annuity of £100 (1827)—Makes an excursion with his
   daughter and Coleridge into Flanders (1828)—Visits Ireland
   (1829)—His eldest son marries (1830)—Visits Sir Walter
   Scott at Abbotsford (1831)—Death of Scott (1832).

APART from the disfavour with which, almost uni-
formly, his publications were received, the existence
of Wordsworth at Rydal Mount must have been
exceptionally happy. He was blest in the pos-
session of a true, loving, and consoling wife, to
whom he could at all times turn—and not in vain—
for wholesome advice and guidance, and for the
comfort and solace which every human heart requires.

She was one on whom, in his misgivings, he could lean for support—the one was truly the complement of the other. How he loved this gentle, amiable lady we may never fully know; but he tells us, in delicate verse, that she was 'dearer far than light and life are dear.' Then, he had spared to him three children—two sons and one daughter—who were growing up like olive branches round about his table, and who were the joy of his being. His sister, too, resided under his roof; and no words can tell what a rich blessing—what a ministering angel —she, through life, was to him. Surely no brother and sister were ever more ardently attached the one to the other: 'Like Juno's swans'—while health permitted — 'still they went coupled and inseparable.'

His sister-in-law, Sarah Hutchinson, continued to make her abode at Rydal Mount; and all were strongly united in the bonds of sincere and lasting affection. They were indeed a happy family.

. One can readily imagine the feelings of pleasure with which the poet would pace backwards and forwards on the green-sward composing his verses, or wander listlessly about the grounds and gardens, bright with the beauty and sweet with the fragrance of a thousand flowers. But, alas! the scented atmosphere had, in one respect, less charms for him than for others. He had no sense of smell.

With reference to this peculiarity, Southey writes:

'Once, and once only, in his life, the dormant power awakened; it was by a bed of stocks in full bloom, at a house which he inhabited in Dorsetshire, some five-and-twenty years ago; and he says it was like a vision of Paradise to him: but it lasted only a few minutes, and the faculty has continued torpid from that time.'

The poet's nephew, in his 'Memoirs,' states, that the perception thus alluded to by Southey was imaginary. 'The incident,' he says, 'occurred at Racedown, when he was walking with Miss H——, who, coming suddenly upon a parterre of sweet flowers, expressed her pleasure at their fragrance,—a pleasure which he caught from her lips, and then fancied to be his own.' Let us not, however, begrudge the poet the benefit of the doubt.

Leigh Hunt, in his charming 'Autobiography,' has given us a partial portrait of Wordsworth, who visited him in London in 1815. The two poets did not meet after this for thirty years, when Wordsworth would be about seventy-five. Writing of Wordsworth's appearance in later life, he says: 'But certainly I never beheld eyes that looked so inspired or supernatural. They were like fires half burning, half smouldering, with a sort of acrid fixture of regard, and seated at the further end of two caverns. One might imagine Ezekiel or Isaiah to have had such eyes.'

During the prolonged period of Wordsworth's

residence at Rydal Mount—thirty-seven years—he
enjoyed the esteem of a choice and magic circle
of friends.   Southey, his brother-poet, lived and
died at Keswick ; De Quincey, for twenty years,
resided at Dove Cottage ; Coleridge continued his
attached friend until removed by death in 1834 ;
Professor Wilson, who did so much to establish his
fame, abode at Elleray, a delightful spot on the
banks of Windermere ; Arnold, of Rugby, was
beautifully located at Fox Howe ; while Hartley
Coleridge dwelt at Nab Cottage, close to the margin
of Grasmere.   Dr. Watson, the Bishop of Llandaff,
was settled at Windermere, and Charles Lloyd at
Brathay.   These, which are some of the names with
which the district is imperishably associated, are verily
names to ' conjure with ;' and there are many others
with whom the poet for years maintained terms of
great intimacy ; amongst whom must be mentioned
Sir Walter Scott, Charles and Mary Lamb, who
were wedded to London, Henry Crabb Robinson,
Haydon the painter, Hazlitt, Mrs. Hemans, and
others.   It was surely something to live for, to
number amongst his friends such worthies as these.
Blair's apostrophe is well known :

> ' Friendship ! mysterious cement of the soul !
> Sweet'ner of life ! and solder of society !'

The year 1816 was notable for the publication
of Wordsworth's 'Ode,' January 18th, 1816, the
day appointed for a general thanksgiving on the ter-

mination of the great European war. In this year also, his eldest brother, Richard, who was an attorney-at-law in London, died, the mournful event taking place on the 19th of May.

In 1819 appeared 'Peter Bell; a Tale in Verse,' dedicated to Robert Southey. This poem, which had been written as far back as 1798, is a remarkable lucubration, and it was a bold undertaking on the part of the poet to publish it. Not but that it was as perfect as he could render it. He had taken infinite pains 'to make the production less unworthy of a favourable reception; or, rather, to fit it for filling *permanently* a station, however humble, in the literature of our country.' It is, perhaps, the most unique of all his poems—the most Wordsworthian. But the story is simple in the extreme. Peter Bell, the hero of the tale, is a potter by trade, as coarse and vicious a man almost as it would be possible to conceive. Although he had trudged about for some thirty years from place to place, and had seen much of the beauties of nature, yet he was as insensible to their influence as a stone. He had sunk below the level of the brute creation. But a change is in store for him; he is to be converted. He is made to witness, on a moon-lit night, the fidelity of an ass to its drowned master, whose body lies in a river, on the banks of which the poor animal had stood for four days and nights without breaking its fast, gazing fixedly into the water. The potter is impressed, and eventually becomes 'a good and honest man.'

We belong to those who see in this work the conception and skill of a great artist. We would not willingly let 'Peter Bell' die. The poem, to our mind, is beautifully and powerfully worked out, and contains many fine passages, which have become 'familiar in our mouths as household words.' Still, it was clamorously assailed by the critics, notably in the *London Monthly Review* and the *London Literary Gazette*. *Blackwood*, however, reviewed it favourably. But in spite of the ridicule that was showered upon it, it was more in demand than any of Wordsworth's previous publications, the five hundred copies struck off in April being followed in May by a second edition. It led to several parodies—'Peter Bell; a Lyrical Ballad,' and 'The Dead Asses; a Lyrical Ballad,' both published in 1819. Shelley also parodied the poem in his 'Peter Bell the Third.' After all, it was no small honour, perhaps, to be satirized by so lofty and ethereal a genius as Shelley. It did Wordsworth no harm. The parody, however, did not appear during Shelley's lifetime, nor indeed for many years after his death, it being printed in 1839.

It was not a little singular that, shortly before the publication of Wordsworth's poem referred to, a burlesque bearing the same name was issued, from the pen of John Hamilton Reynolds. As it has never been our good fortune to come across this composition, we can offer no opinion with regard to its merits.

'The Waggoner,' by Wordsworth, was also published in the same year as 'Peter Bell,' with a gratifying dedication to Charles Lamb, in which the poet says : 'When I sent you, a few weeks ago, the "Tale of Peter Bell," you asked why "The Waggoner" was not added ?' The poem had been read to Lamb in manuscript in or about the year 1806, and, judging from the fact that he had remembered it so clearly, he must have been considerably impressed with it. The success of the volume, which comprised, in addition to the story, a number of sonnets, was small indeed, and the reason is not far to seek—the incidents and descriptions being altogether local. Neither is there much, if any, true conception in the poem. Its publication did not add one leaf to the poet's bays. 'Nobody, we are sure,' said *Blackwood*, 'who might have seen it published anonymously, would have suspected it to be a production of the Great Poet of the Lakes.' And the *London Monthly Review* stated : 'Mr. Wordsworth appears determined to try how far he can trample on the degraded poetry of his country. "Keep it down," seems to be his prevailing principle ; and well may he add, "Now it is down."' Macaulay, writing of Byron, in the *Edinburgh Review*, says, that 'Peter Bell excited his (Byron's) spleen to such a degree, that he apostrophized the shades of Pope and Dryden, and demanded of them whether it were possible that such trash could evade contempt :'

> " Pedlars," and " boats," and " waggons !'' Oh ! ye shades
> Of Pope and Dryden, are we come to this ?'

This work also was parodied—'Benjamin the Waggoner, a Ryghte Merrie and Conceitede Tale in Verse ; a Fragment,' appearing in the same year. Of this travesty, the *London Monthly Review* remarked : ' We must observe that the parody, although it is entitled " Benjamin the Waggoner," is all about Peter Bell.'

Of all Wordsworth's poems published after 1800, 'The Waggoner' could, perhaps, be best spared ; and, although we treasure every one of his performances, it must frankly be admitted that it is far from being a lofty flight of genius. Sir Walter Scott wonders ' why Wordsworth will sometimes choose to crawl upon all-fours, when God has given him so noble a countenance to lift to heaven.' Sir Walter, it need scarcely be added, had, in general, an exalted opinion of ' the amiable bard of Rydal,' as he was pleased to style Wordsworth. ' The Waggoner' was written at Dove Cottage, Grasmere, which, as previously intimated, had formerly seen service as an inn ; and the poem contains a notable reference to Wordsworth, which we subjoin :

> ' There, where the Dove and Olive-bough
> Once hung, a poet harbours now,—
> A simple water-drinking bard.'

Such was Wordsworth. He was decidedly a man of humble tastes, but of high and ennobling aspirations. Even in the matter of dress, notwithstanding that on his going to Cambridge, according to De Quincey, he had ' actually assumed the beau, or, in modern slang, the " dandy," ' dressing in silk stockings, with his hair powdered, he was in more advanced life far from fastidious ; and some have not hesitated to describe him as slovenly in this respect. But the fact of his living in retirement should not be overlooked. Besides, it was his custom to take out-of-door exercise in all states of the weather, and many a severe wetting did he encounter in his walks and rambles far and wide. William Howitt, at all times a welcome visitor to the Wordsworths, has given us the following interesting account of the poet : ' He was,' he says, ' with all his solemnity and his poetry, a plain man. He did not walk his mountains in stilts, but in good hob-nailed shoes, often with a gray shepherd's plaid on his shoulders, and a broad straw hat or a simple cloth cap on his head. You might have taken him for a good, honest old countryman, and it would only be by entering into conversation with him that you would discover the man of great mind.'

That poetry was to Wordsworth the business of

his life, is abundantly evidenced not only by the large and varied amount he produced, but also, we think, by the appearance in the following year (1820) of 'The River Duddon, a Series of Sonnets; Vaudracour and Julia; and other Poems: to which is annexed a Topographical Description of the Country of the Lakes in the North of England,' the book consisting of upwards of 300 pages. The sonnets and other pieces in this volume were dedicated to the poet's brother, the Rev. Dr. Wordsworth, then rector of the parish of Lambeth, in a beautifully-written introductory poem, which cannot be read too often. Of the sonnets, perhaps the best known of the series is the concluding one, entitled 'After-Thought,' commencing,

'I thought of thee, my partner and my guide,'

which is an exquisite and powerful composition—one of the finest in the whole range of sonnet literature. In 'Vaudracour and Julia,' a thrilling episode, Wordsworth has painted an inimitable picture of the master passion—love, in which he has risen almost, if not fully, to the style and strength of the greatest Elizabethan dramatists. No apology need be made for its insertion.

'His present mind
Was under fascination ;—he beheld
A vision, and adored the thing he saw.
Arabian fiction never filled the world
With half the wonders that were wrought for him.
Earth breathed in one great presence of the spring ;

Life turned the meanest of her implements,
Before his eyes, to price above all gold ;
The house she dwelt in was a sainted shrine ;
Her chamber-window did surpass in glory
The portals of the dawn ; all paradise
Could, by the simple opening of a door,
Let itself in upon him :—pathways, walks,
Swarmed with enchantment, till his spirit sank,
Surcharged, within him,—overblest to move
Beneath a sun that wakes a weary world
To its dull round of ordinary cares ;
A man too happy for mortality !'

The 'Description of the Country of the Lakes,'
included in the volume, had originally been published in 1810, and has already been noticed.
This work ran through numerous editions during
the author's lifetime.

In the summer of 1820, Wordsworth, accompanied
by his wife and sister and some friends, proceeded
to Switzerland and Italy, the tour occupying about
four months.   At Lucerne, Henry Crabb Robinson
became one of the party.   Amongst many places of
interest visited by the poet on this occasion, were
Bruges, Cologne, Heidelburg, Chamouny, and the
Field of Waterloo.   On the return of the tourists
from Boulogne, they had a narrow escape from
shipwreck, the vessel striking upon a sand-bank, and
being afterwards stranded.   This incident, of course,
gave rise to a sonnet.   When in London, Wordsworth had the pleasure of meeting several attached
friends—Rogers the poet, Charles and Mary Lamb,
Talfourd, and others.   He paid a visit to his beloved

friend Coleridge, on the 18th of November. After visiting—with his wife and sister—his brother, Dr. Wordsworth, at Cambridge, whither he had been promoted, and Sir George and Lady Beaumont at Coleorton, the poet returned with his company to Rydal Mount, which he reached on Christmas Eve.

An accident, which barely escaped proving fatal, befell Wordsworth in May, 1822. He was progressing with some friends towards Haweswater, when he had the misfortune to be thrown violently from his horse, sustaining considerable injury to his head. On examination, it was thought that the skull was fractured, but fortunately such was not the case, the wound which at first appeared so alarming turning out to be merely superficial, with some abrasion of the bone, caused by the sharp-pointed stone against which he fell. Thanks to the strength of constitution and temperate habits of the poet, he recovered with a rapidity that surprised his friends.

As might be expected, his travels in Switzerland and Italy furnished some noble inspirations, which were given to the world in 1822, under the title of 'Memorials of a Tour on the Continent, 1820.'

In 1822, Wordsworth also published the 'Ecclesiastical Sketches,' since called Sonnets. These had been suggested during his visit to Sir George Beaumont, who contemplated the erection of a new church on his charming estate. The volume, which contains some truly elegant sonnets, of which those on 'Walton's Book of Lives,' and 'Inside of King's College Chapel, Cambridge,' are, perhaps, the most widely-known and admired, was highly reviewed in *Blackwood's Magazine ;* but, like Wordsworth's previous publications, it was severely condemned by Jeffrey, in the *Edinburgh Review.*

A confirmed traveller, the poet, together with his wife, in the spring of 1823, made a tour in Belgium and Holland. He was then greatly troubled with an affection of the eyes, which happily passed away. In the following year, he found himself on a ramble in North Wales, where he spent some days with his college friend, the Rev. Robert Jones, then a curate in the Church of England, the poet's wife and daughter, Dora, being of the party.

On Wordsworth's return to Rydal Mount after his excursions, his neighbours more than once remarked: 'Well, there he is ; we are glad to hear him *booing* about again.' This was in allusion to his habit of composing and murmuring his verses in the open air. He himself has told us, that 'One day a stranger, having walked round the garden and grounds of Rydal Mount, asked of one of the female servants, who happened to be at the door, permission to see her master's study. " This," said she, leading him forward, " is my master's *library*, where he keeps his books ; but his *study* is out of doors." ' His library, properly so-called, was about as scanty and wretched an affair as any literary man could

well be imagined to possess, consisting of but some
three to five hundred books—a heterogeneous collection in tattered condition, which occupied only a
few shelves.   Southey, on the other hand, had one
of the finest and most valuable private libraries in
the kingdom, leaving behind him at his death some
fourteen thousand volumes.   But Southey was a
marvellous reader, while Wordsworth was less a
reader of books than of the great volume of nature,
which lay before him like an open scroll.   In the
words of a modern poetical writer : 'Nature to him
presented one broad beautiful view, a page of poetry
written by the hand of God Himself.'   'As to
buying books,' says Wordsworth, writing in 1819,
'I can affirm that in *new* books I have not spent
five shillings for the last five years,' and he adds—
and this is significant in his case—'small and paltry
as my collection is, I have not read a fifth part of
it.'   Probably he would have been a 'fuller' man,
and one of broader sympathies, had he read more.
As Matthew Arnold, the foremost critic of the nineteenth century, declares : 'The one thing wanting to
make Wordsworth an even greater poet than he is,
—his thought richer, and his influence of wider
application,—was that he should have read more
books, among them, no doubt, those of that Goethe
whom he disparaged without reading him.'   Wordsworth was a maker, rather than a reader of books.
And a good deal of his delightful philosophy is

contained in the following lines from 'The Tables Turned :'

> 'Come forth into the light of things,
>   Let Nature be your teacher.
>   *   *   *   *
>   One impulse from a vernal wood
>   May teach you more of man,
>   Of moral evil and of good,
>   Than all the sages can.'

It is narrated that Wordsworth once observed to Rogers, that Southey, in advancing age, had left off reading to a large extent, and that he principally read his own books.

'Why, it is very natural that he should do so,' said Rogers; 'I read my works oftener than any others, and I dare say that you do the same.'

'Yes, that he does,' said Mrs. Wordsworth; 'you know you do, William.'

Like Rogers, he was continually altering his poems—not unfrequently to their disadvantage. It is remarkable that, while he frequently omitted, he seldom added anything to his compositions. To the philological student, Professor Knight's recent edition of Wordsworth is simply invaluable, inasmuch as it contains the numerous variorum readings of the poems, from their first appearance down to 1849, the year immediately preceding the poet's death.

On the 7th of February, 1827, Wordsworth, to his lasting sorrow, lost his attached friend Sir George Beaumont, who died in his seventy-third year, and was buried at Coleorton. If any further proof were needed to show the great esteem in which the deceased nobleman held the poet, it is to be found in the fact that, ever mindful of his interests, he bequeathed him an annuity of £100, in order that he might the better enjoy a yearly tour.

The summer of 1828 found Wordsworth and his daughter, accompanied by Coleridge, on an excursion into Flanders. After spending a fortnight on the banks of the Rhine, they returned by way of Holland.

In the autumn of the following year, Wordsworth paid a visit to Ireland, in the company of Mr. J. Marshall, M.P. for Leeds.

On the 11th of October, 1830, the Rev. John Wordsworth, the poet's eldest son, then Rector of Moresby, entered the holy state of matrimony, marrying the daughter of Henry Curwen, of Workington Hall, Cumberland.

In 1831, the poet and his daughter set off in the autumn for Scotland, to see Sir Walter Scott, who was then in ruined circumstances, and in feeble health both of body and mind, and was about to proceed to Italy. Wordsworth was at this time suffering from inflammation in his eyes, over which he wore a deep green shade, and was otherwise far from well.

'How sadly changed,' says he, 'did I find him from the man I had seen so healthy, gay, and hope-

ful a few years before, when he said at the inn at
Paterdale, in my presence, his daughter Anne also
being there, with Mr. Lockhart, my own wife and
daughter, and Mr. Quillinan, " I mean to live till I
am *eighty!* and shall write as long as I live. . . ."
The inmates and guests we found there were Sir
Walter, Major Scott, Anne Scott, and Mr. and Mrs.
Lockhart ; Mr. Liddell, his lady and brother, and
Mr. Allan the painter, and Mr. Laidlaw, a very
old friend of Sir Walter's. . . . In the evening, Mr.
and Mrs. Liddell sang, and Mrs. Lockhart chanted
old ballads to her harp ; and Mr. Allan, hanging
over the back of a chair, told and acted odd stories
in a humorous way.   With this exhibition, and his
daughter's singing, Sir Walter was much amused,
and, indeed, were we all, as far as circumstances
would allow.   On Tuesday morning, Sir Walter Scott
accompanied us, and most of the party, to Newark
Castle, on the Yarrow.   When we alighted from
the carriages, he walked pretty stoutly, and had
great pleasure in revisiting these his favourite haunts.
Of that excursion, the verses, " Yarrow Revisited "
are a memorial. . . .   On our return in the after-
noon, we had to cross the Tweed, directly opposite
Abbotsford. . . .   A rich, but sad light, of rather
a purple than a golden hue, was spread over the
Eildon Hills at that moment ; and, thinking it
probable that it might be the last time Sir Walter
would cross the stream, I was not a little moved,

and expressed some of my feelings in the sonnet
beginning,

"A trouble, not of clouds," etc.

At noon on Thursday we left Abbotsford, and, on
the morning of that day, Sir Walter and I had a
serious conversation, *tête-à-tête*, when he spoke with
gratitude of the happy life which, upon the whole,
he had led. He had written in my daughter's
album, before he came into the breakfast-room that
morning, a few stanzas addressed to her ; and, while
putting the book into her hand, in his own study,
standing by his desk, he said to her in my presence,
" I should not have done anything of this kind, but
for your father's sake ; they are probably the last
verses I shall ever write." They show how much
his mind was impaired ; not by the strain of
thought, but by the execution—some of the lines
being imperfect, and one stanza wanting correspond-
ing rhymes. One letter, the initial S, had been
omitted in the spelling of his own name.'

The poets parted that day ; and what occurred
afterwards is well known. After visiting Naples,
Pompeii, Rome, and other places, the 'Great
Unknown,' on going down the Rhine, was stricken
by a further attack of apoplectic paralysis. He
was brought to London, and ultimately reached
Abbotsford.

'About half-past one p.m.,' says his biographer,

'on the 21st of September, 1832, Sir Walter
breathed his last, in the presence of all his children.
It was a beautiful day—so warm that every window
was wide open—and so perfectly still that the sound
of all others most delicious to his ear, the gentle
ripple of the Tweed over its pebbles, was distinctly
audible as we knelt around the bed, and his eldest
son kissed and closed his eyes.'

CHAPTER X.

'How wonderful is Death !
Death and his brother Sleep.'
Shelley.

Wordsworth visits the Isle of Man *en route* for Scotland (1833)—Poems and incidents relating to the Island— Coleridge dies (25th July, 1834) — Charles Lamb dies (27th Dec., 1834)—Loses several friends by death (1835) —'Yarrow Revisited, and other Poems' (1835)—'Evening Voluntaries'—His alleged Pantheism—Sarah Hutchinson dies (1836)—Visits Italy (1837)—'The Sonnets of William Wordsworth' (1838)—University of Oxford confers D.C.L. upon him (1839) — Is acknowledged to be the greatest living poet—Is visited by Mrs. Sigourney (1840)—His darling daughter, Dora, marries Edward Quillinan (1841)— Classified collection of his poems in six volumes (1842)— 'Poems : chiefly of Early and Late Years, including "The Borderers, a Tragedy "' (1842)—Resigns the Distributor- ship of Stamps—Is awarded by the Crown a pension of £300 per annum.

IN the summer of 1833, Wordsworth and his son, the Rev. John Wordsworth, accompanied by Henry Crabb Robinson, made a tour in Scotland, proceed- ing by way of Whitehaven and the Isle of Man, where a few days were enjoyably passed. That the poet was greatly pleased with the Island (where this biography is penned) is amply demonstrated by the various sonnets referring to Manxland which were suggested or composed during the excursion. Wordsworth was not slow to observe what is one of the most attractive features in connection with this delightful watering-place, a foot-note to the charming sonnet, ' By the Sea-shore,' reading : ' The sea-water on the coast of the Isle of Man is singularly pure and beautiful.'   It would have been indeed inconceivable had he not been struck with the serene beauty of the picturesque

> ' Gem of the ocean ! lovely Mona's Isle !
> Fairest of emeralds rising from the sea !'

The sonnet on ' Tynwald Hill,' where, in ancient times, the kings of Man were enthroned, and where to this day the local Acts of Tynwald are promulgated annually with great ceremony on the 5th of July, elicited the following remarks from Wordsworth : ' Mr. Robinson and I,' says he, ' walked the greater part of the way from Castletown to Peel, and stopped some time at Tynwald Hill.   One of our companions was an elderly man, who, in a muddy way, for he was tipsy, explained and answered, as far as he could, my inquiries about this place, and the ceremonies held here.   I found more agreeable company in some little children, one of whom, upon my request, recited the Lord's Prayer to me, and I helped her to a clearer understanding of it as well as I could ; but I was not at all satisfied with my own part—hers was much better done ; and I am persuaded that, like other children, she knew more about it than she was able to express, especially to a stranger.' One can fancy the aged author of ' We are Seven ' (God love him !)—he was then sixty-three—not disdaining, in his characteristic humility, to hold converse with the little girl, whom he had never before seen, and to unfold to her eager ears the beauties of the universal prayer. Verily, as he himself says : ' Every great poet is a teacher.'   It were a great pity did this individual die without learning who the amiable stranger was.   She may yet be living.   What would not we, who love the poet as with an intense personal affection, have given to have changed places with her !

From the Isle of Man, Wordsworth and his party went on to Scotland, where further poetical fruit was produced.

On the 25th of July, 1834, Samuel Taylor Coleridge, ' Logician, Metaphysician, Bard,' as Charles Lamb delighted to call him, ' shuffled off this mortal coil,' passing away at his friend Mr. Gillman's, at Highgate, where he had found an asylum for the last nineteen years of his life.   He had, with the shadow of certain death over him, written his epitaph the year before :

' Stop, Christian passer-by :—Stop, child of God,
    And read, with gentle breast.   Beneath this sod

A poet lies, or that which once seemed he—
O, lift one thought in prayer for S. T. C.—
That he who many a year with toil of breath
Found death in life may here find life in death !
Mercy for praise,—to be forgiven for fame,—
He asked, and hoped, through Christ.   Do thou the same.'

He was buried in Highgate churchyard, and a
marble tablet in the new church bears an inscription
which speaks in eulogistic strains of 'this pious and
exalted Christian.'

Six months afterwards, Lamb, whose grief on the
death of his friend was so great that he seems never
to have fully rallied from it, continually giving vent
to the exclamation, 'Coleridge is dead ! Coleridge
is dead !' died on the 27th of December, from the
result of an unfortunate accident; and who can
doubt that he speedily rejoined the gifted dreamer—
who, if ever poet did, 'drank the milk of Paradise'
—in that better land

'Where spirits blend,
And friend holds fellowship with friend'?

In the following year also, death was busy, the
Rev. Robert Jones, one of Wordsworth's earliest
and dearest friends; Mrs. Hemans, who had spent
the summer of 1830 at the Dove's Nest, on the
banks of Windermere ; and James Hogg, 'the
Ettrick Shepherd,' departing this life ; and the
sorrow of the meditative poet about this period
may indeed be better imagined than put into

11

words. Alas! Wordsworth could truly exclaim, with Blair,

> 'On this side, and on that, men see their friends
> Drop off, like leaves in autumn;'

and he gave expression to his feelings in an exquisite 'Extempore Effusion upon the Death of James Hogg.'

> 'Like clouds that rake the mountain-summits,
>   Or waves that own no curbing hand,
> How fast has brother followed brother,
>   From sunshine to the sunless land!
>
> Yet I, whose lids from infant slumber
>   Were earlier raised, remain to hear
> A timid voice, that asks in whispers,
>   "Who next will drop and disappear   '

In the beginning of the same year (1835), Wordsworth published a volume, entitled 'Yarrow Revisited, and other Poems,' the tours made in Scotland in 1831 and 1833 having suggested the material. The collection, which was dedicated to the poet Rogers, was commended by the *London Athenæum*, the *London Literary Gazette*, and also by *Blackwood*. Writing to Wordsworth on the 9th of May, Southey says: 'Thank you for your new volume, which it is needless for me to praise. It will do good now and hereafter; more and more as it shall be more and more widely read; and there is no danger of its ever being laid on the shelf.'

The beautiful poems to which Wordsworth gave

the name of 'Evening Voluntaries,' were, for the
most part, composed between 1832 and 1835. In
these charming compositions, the poet appears in all
the humility and serenity of his character; touches
of melancholy are here and there discernible, but
confidence and faith predominate, and the dominant
note is hope.   With Wordsworth at this time,
the evening shadows of life were descending—the
day was far spent.   How doubly sweet, therefore,
is it to find him penning such noble lines as these !
He is addressing the Supreme Power:

> 'Whatever discipline Thy will ordain
>   For the brief course that must for me remain ;
>   Teach me with quick-eared spirit to rejoice
>   In admonitions of Thy softest voice !
>   Whate'er the path these mortal feet may trace,
>   Breathe through my soul the blessing of Thy grace,
>   Glad, through a perfect love, a faith sincere
>   Drawn from the wisdom that begins with fear,
>   Glad to expand ; and, for a season, free
>   From finite cares, to rest absorbed in Thee !'

The poem from which these lines are taken was
composed on Easter Sunday, April 7, 1833, the
poet's sixty-third birthday.

In another of the 'Voluntaries,' beginning,

> 'Not in the lucid intervals of life,'

he says :

> ' Meekness is the cherished bent
>   Of all the truly great and all the innocent.
>
> But who *is* innocent ?   By grace divine,
>   Not otherwise, O Nature ! we are thine,
>   Through good and evil thine, in just degree
>   Of rational and manly sympathy.'

11—2

And, lastly, in a melodious inspiration, ' By the Side of Rydal Mere,' he asserts:

> ' The wisest, happiest, of our kind are they
> That ever walk content with Nature's way,
> God's goodness—measuring bounty as it may ;
> For whom the gravest thought of what they miss,
> Chastening the fulness of a present bliss,
> Is with that wholesome office satisfied,
> While unrepining sadness is allied
> In thankful bosoms to a modest pride.'

Those who maintain, without the slightest warrant, that Wordsworth's god was Nature, and that he was Pantheistic in his belief, would do well to note these and numberless kindred passages in his writings, and 'read, mark, learn, and inwardly digest them.' Not but that he did frequently, for poetical purposes, present only the Pantheistic side or aspect of a subject, which hosts of other poets have done, and, no doubt, will continue to do, till verse shall be no more. But we must relegate to the concluding chapter our further remarks on this head.

On the 23rd of June, 1836, a heavy affliction befell the happy household at Rydal Mount. This was the decease of Sarah Hutchinson, Wordsworth's sister-in-law, a person,' says his nephew, ' of cultivated mind, sound judgment, refined taste, tender affections, firm religious principle, and fervent piety.' This amiable lady, whose remains were buried in Grasmere churchyard, had long resided beneath the poet's hospitable roof, and was almost as dear to him as though she had been his own sister.   But Death is no respecter of persons. Wordsworth was strangely outliving the most of his friends, and sorrow had long since set its sanctifying seal upon his brow.

In March, 1837, he set out from London, together with Henry Crabb Robinson, *en route* for Italy. 'During my whole life,' he says, 'I had felt a strong desire to visit Rome, and the other celebrated cities and regions of Italy.'   The travellers returned in August, after a delightful excursion of five months. With reference to this tour, Henry Crabb Robinson says: ' I have been often asked whether Mr. W. wrote anything on the journey, and my answer has always been, "Little or nothing."   Seeds were cast into the earth, and they took root slowly.   This reminds me that I once was privy to the conception of a sonnet, with a distinctness which did not once occur on the longer Italian journey.   This was when I accompanied him into the Isle of Man.   We had been drinking tea with Mr. and Mrs. Cookson, and left them when the weather was dull.   Very soon after leaving them we passed the church-tower of Bala Sala (Ballasalla).   The upper part of the tower had a sort of frieze of yellow lichens.   Mr. W. pointed it out to me, and said, "It's a perpetual sunshine."   I thought no more of it, till I read the beautiful sonnet :

'"Broken in fortune, but in mind entire."'

The seeds were indeed cast into the earth; and, although the harvest was not soon given to the world, Wordsworth was busy in imparting poetic life to the materials he had accumulated on his travels.

A very important publication, which it would be a great oversight to omit, appeared in 1838. This was 'The Sonnets of William Wordsworth; Collected in One Volume; with a Few Additional Ones now First Published.' The work consisted of 477 pages, octavo. 'No one, since Milton,' said the *London Literary Gazette*, 'has so adorned our language in this species of composition.' The book was favourably reviewed in many quarters—how could it be otherwise? 'Of all authors,' says Sir Egerton Brydges, 'Wordsworth has most succeeded in this department.'

In the summer of 1839, the University of Oxford honoured the aged poet by conferring upon him the degree of D.C.L., the Latin oration being delivered by the Rev. John Keble, then Professor of Poetry, who justly claimed, 'that he (Wordsworth) had shed a celestial light upon the affections, the occupations, the piety of the poor.' The tide was now turning rapidly in favour of Wordsworth. Longfellow has well said, that 'all things come round to him who will but wait.' And Wordsworth had waited long and patiently for the tardy wreaths of fame that were now and henceforth to be freely showered upon him. As we have thought, in penning this brief biography, of the unfavourable receptions accorded, in general, to the numerous publications of Wordsworth, we have been forcibly reminded of the pungent exclamation of Charles Lamb, on the rejection of one of his sonnets : 'Hang the age ! I will write for Antiquity.' The fact is, Wordsworth was outliving his critics, and a younger generation of admirers was springing up about him, and in their hands his reputation was safe—his immortality was assured.   Jeffrey, however, was not yet dead, and it must have been intensely disappointing to him to find his strictures, which had checked—how largely none can tell, the power of the *Edinburgh Review* being so tremendous—the popularity of the poet, regarded as conclusive evidence of his utter incapacity, and want of insight and discernment, as a poetical critic.   It was the good fortune of that young but remarkable Christian minister and philanthropist, Frederick William Robertson, during a short university career, to witness the ceremony referred to.   He says : 'Scarcely had his name been pronounced, than from three thousand voices at once there broke forth a burst of applause, echoed and taken up again and again when it seemed about to die away, and that thrice repeated—a cry in which

  ' " Old England's heart and voice unite,
     Whether she hail the wine cup or the fight,
     Or bid each hand be strong, or bid each heart be light."

' There were young eyes there, filled with an emotion

of which they had no need to be ashamed; there
were hearts beating with the proud feeling of triumph,
that, at last, the world had recognised the merit of
the man they had loved so long, and acknowledged
as their teacher; and yet, when that noise was pro-
tracted, there came a reaction in their feelings, and
they began to perceive that *that* was not, after all,
the true reward and recompense for all that Wordsworth had done for England: it seemed as if all that
noise was vulgarizing the poet; it seemed more
natural and desirable to think of him afar off in
his simple dales and mountains, the high-priest of
Nature, weaving in honoured poverty his songs to
liberty and truth, than to see him there clad in a
scarlet robe and bespattered with applause.'

Wordsworth was now looked upon far and wide
as the greatest living poet. For years past, the
clouds which had for so long obscured his fame had
been dispersing; and it is gratifying to record, that
the honour bestowed upon him by the University of
Oxford was but a foretaste of better things to come.
'Thus the whirligig of time brings in his revenges.'

In the summer of 1840, Mrs. Sigourney, the most
charming of American poetesses, paid a visit to
Wordsworth at Rydal Mount, of which she has
given us a vivid account in her 'Pleasant Memories
of Pleasant Lands.' She says:

'Though I had more earnestly desired to see him
(Wordsworth) than almost any distinguished writer,

whom from early life had been admired, it was with
a degree of diffidence, amounting almost to trepida-
tion, that I accepted the invitation to his house,
which had been left at the inn. As I approached
his lovely and unpretending habitation, embowered
with ivy and roses, I felt that to go into the presence
of Europe's loftiest crowned head would not cost so
much effort as to approach and endeavour to converse
with a king in the realm of mind. But the kindness
of his reception and that of his family, and the un-
ceremonious manner in which they make a guest
feel as one of them, removed the reserve and un-
easiness of a stranger's heart.

'Wordsworth is past seventy years of age, and
has the same full, expanded brow which we see in
his busts and engravings. His conversation has that
simplicity and richness for which you are prepared
by his writings. He led me around his grounds,
pointing out the improvements which he had made
during the last thirty years, and the trees, hedges,
and shrubbery, which had been planted under his
direction. Snatches of the gorgeous scenery of lake
and mountain were visible from different points;
and one of the walks terminated with the near view
of a chapel built by his neighbour, the Lady Elizabeth Fleming, on whose domain are both the upper
and lower falls of Rydal Water. In this beautiful
combination of woods, cliffs, and waters, and solemn
temple pointing to the skies, we see the germ of

many of his thrilling descriptions; for his habit is to compose in the open air. He loves the glorious scenery of his native region, and is evidently pleased when others admire it.

'His household consists of a wife, sister, two sons, and a daughter. The eldest of the sons is married, and, with a group of five children, resides under the same roof; giving to the family a pleasant, patriarchal aspect. . . . It was delightful to see so eminent a poet, thus pursuing the calm tenor of a happy life, surrounded by all those domestic affections and charities which his pure lays have done so much to cherish in the hearts of others.'

In May, 1841, Dora, the only surviving and darling daughter of the poet, was wedded to Edward Quillinan, son of a merchant of Oporto. Though born at Oporto, he was educated in England, and had long been an intense admirer of Wordsworth's poetry. On quitting the army in 1821, he had fixed his abode in the vale of Rydal, in order that he might more fully enjoy his society. Mr. Quillinan had been previously married to a daughter of Sir Egerton Brydges, by whom he had two children, both girls. Some idea of the affectionate nature and disposition of Dora Wordsworth may be gathered from the fact that she became, on the death of their parent, almost as a mother to the little ones, whom she had intimately known, and dearly loved, from infancy. After their marriage, which was celebrated at Bath, where Wordsworth and his family were on a visit to a friend, Mr. Quillinan and his new bride resided in Canterbury, and subsequently in London; but, doubtless to be near their loved ones, they settled near Rydal in the winter of 1843-44.

The year 1842 was a highly important one in the life of Wordsworth. He now issued a classified collection of his works, which extended to six octavo volumes, his poetical pieces being arranged, according to the nature of the subjects, under the heads of 'Poems referring to the Period of Childhood,' 'Poems founded on the Affections,' 'Poems of the Fancy,' 'Poems of the Imagination,' etc. The classification is of necessity more or less arbitrary and unsatisfactory, and it does not seem to commend itself to the general reader, who cannot be credited with the poetic insight which guided the poet in thus arranging the poems. For ourselves, we would prefer reprints, so far as the order is concerned, of the several publications of Wordsworth, giving together the contents of each volume as it appeared, subject, of course, to the corrections and alterations made by the author. But failing this, the scholarly, and in every respect most admirable edition by Professor Knight, in which the poems are printed in the order in which they were written, leaves nothing to be desired. Indeed, it is doubtful whether this arrangement be not after all the best that could be devised, enabling the student, as it does, to follow more closely the development of the poet's mind and poetical theories; though it places him at no inconsiderable disadvantage with regard to the reviews accorded to the various volumes, to which we attach, in the case of Wordsworth, more than ordinary importance. Be this as it may, Professor Knight has well earned the gratitude of every lover of Wordsworth, and he will assuredly go down to posterity holding in his hand his edition of the works of the great poet-teacher.

In this year, Wordsworth also published his last volume, entitled 'Poems: chiefly of Early and Late Years, including the Borderers, a Tragedy.' This publication, amongst much other matter, included 'Guilt and Sorrow; or, Incidents on Salisbury Plain,' and numerous compositions suggested by his tour in Italy in 1837.

During the course of the year, he resigned the appointment he had held so long—that of Distributor of Stamps—in favour of his son William, who had acted for some time at Carlisle, as his deputy. His resignation of this office implied the sacrifice of above £500 per annum, and it is, therefore, all the more pleasing to learn, that, towards the close of the same year, he was awarded by the Crown an annual grant of £300, to be paid during his life. Sir Robert Peel, who was then Prime Minister, in the letter in which the proposal was announced, stated: 'I need scarcely add, that the acceptance, by you, of this mark of favour from the Crown, considering the grounds on which it is proposed, will impose no restraint upon your perfect independence, and involve no obligation of a personal nature.' As there has been some misconception with regard to the allowance thus bestowed upon Wordsworth, some asserting that he relinquished his appointment on a retiring pension, it remains to be positively added, that the grant in question was conferred upon him purely in consideration of his eminent literary merit, and had not the remotest reference to his retirement from official life.

CHAPTER XI.

'For blessings ever wait on virtuous deeds,
And though a late, a sure reward succeeds.'
Congreve.

Southey dies (21st March, 1843)—Wordsworth is appointed
Poet Laureate—Jeffrey's 'Essays' republished—Is presented to the Queen (1845)—Reference to Dorothy, his
invalid sister—His brother Christopher dies (1846)—His
younger son marries (1847)—Dora Quillinan dies (9th July,
1847)—Hartley Coleridge dies (1849)—Daily life at Rydal
Mount—Anecdotes of Wordsworth.

On the 21st of March, 1843, Wordsworth's attached
friend Robert Southey, Poet Laureate, breathed
his last, in the sixty-ninth year of his age. He
had never fully recovered the loss he sustained in
the death of his beloved wife, Edith, which occurred
in 1837, after some years of mental and bodily
affliction. His subsequent marriage with Caroline
Bowles, which was, in a measure, rendered necessary,
proved a trying and melancholy one for her, the
mind of the indefatigable poet, biographer, historian,
and miscellaneous writer, which had throughout his
prolonged literary career been seriously overtaxed,
soon afterwards becoming a complete wreck. The

three closing years of his life were passed in a most
deplorable condition. 'His dearly - prized books,'
says his son, 'were a pleasure to him almost to the
end, and he would walk slowly round his library
looking at them, and taking them down mechani-
cally.' Three years before his death, he had failed
to recognise Wordsworth till he was told who his
visitor was. 'Then,' says Wordsworth, 'his eyes
flashed for a moment with their former brightness,
but he sank into the state in which I had found
him, patting with both hands his books affection-
ately, like a child. Having attempted in vain to
interest him by a few observations, I took my leave,
after five minutes or so. It was, for me, a mournful
visit, and for his poor wife also. His health is
good, and he may live many years; though the body
is much enfeebled.'

Alas, poor Southey! Well might those who saw
him exclaim,

> ' O, what a noble mind is here o'erthrown !'

But, as the same immortal bard says,

> ' Men must endure their going hence,
> Even as their coming hither.'

Death, however, at length arrived 'with friendly
care,' and closed the painful scene; and the remains
of this great and remarkable man—who had been
' doing his duty for fifty noble years of labour;
day by day storing up learning; day by day work-

ing for scant wages; most charitable out of his
small means; bravely faithful to the calling which
he had chosen; refusing to turn from his path for
popular praise or prince's favour'—were, on a stormy,
wet morning, consigned to their last resting-place in
the beautiful old churchyard of Crosthwaite. The
aged Wordsworth and his son-in-law, Edward Quillinan, who had come all the way from Rydal, were,
it is stated, the only strangers present. The tombstone bears the following record :

> 'HERE LIES THE BODY OF
> ROBERT   SOUTHEY, LL.D.,
> POET LAUREATE ;
> BORN AUGUST 12, 1774 ;
> DIED MARCH 21, 1843 ;
> FOR FORTY YEARS A RESIDENT IN THIS PARISH.
> ALSO, OF
> E D I T H, HIS WIFE ;
> BORN MAY 20, 1774 ;
> DIED NOV. 16, 1837.'

An imposing full-length recumbent effigy of the
poet, in white marble, by the sculptor Lough, is to be
found within the church. This handsome memorial,
which was erected by public subscription, is graced
on the base by a fitting poetical inscription from the
pen of Wordsworth. The epitaph is included in
his poems.

On the death of Southey, the laurel was rightly bestowed upon Wordsworth. The stricken poet—he was

now in his seventy-fourth year—at first entertained great scruples with regard to the propriety of accepting the honour, and he begged permission to decline it.   The offer, however, which had been conveyed in graceful terms by the Lord Chamberlain, with the hearty concurrence of Sir Robert Peel, and, above all, with the gracious approval of the Queen, was pressed upon him ; and on his being assured that nothing would be required from him, and that it was made in order to pay him ' that tribute of respect which was justly due to the first of living poets,' he cheerfully accepted the distinction—

> ' That wreath which in Eliza's golden days
> . . . . divinest Spenser wore.'

As might be expected, he composed but little after this period.   Indeed, with but one exception, when he wrote his ' Ode on the Installation of Prince Albert at Cambridge,' published in quarto, in 1847, he does not appear to have sounded the lyre in the capacity of Laureate.   But he had, in all justice, already written enough, and that of a quality such as the world will not willingly let die ; and it may without exaggeration be stated, that if ever a poet was worthy of the laurel, that man was William Wordsworth.

In the following year, Jeffrey republished a selection of his ' Essays ' contributed to the *Edinburgh Review ;* and, in doing so, he included but two critiques on Wordsworth—those on ' The Excursion '

12

and 'The White Doe of Rylstone '—to the first o:
which he subjoined a note, in which he acknow
ledged his love for many of the attributes of the
poet's genius, and the respect he bore to his char
acter.

In the *Diary, etc., of Henry Crabb Robinson*
we are told, that 'Empson says he believed Jeffrey's
distaste for Wordsworth to be honest—mere uncon·
geniality of mind.' It was clearly not in the
natural order of things that such a critic should sit
in judgment on Wordsworth, and weigh him in the
balances. His strictures, therefore, must be taken, as
they long have been, for what they are worth. The
words of dear old Izaak Walton, in the preface to
his immortal 'Angler,' may not inaptly be applied to
Jeffrey : 'If thou be a severe, sour-complexioned man,
then I here disallow thee to be a competent judge.'
Charles Lamb had admittedly no ear for music;
however valuable, therefore, his opinions on litera·
ture might be, he never could have posed as a
musical critic.

In 1845, the venerable Laureate was presented to
the Queen, by whom it need scarcely be said he was
most graciously received. It was an affecting sight
to see the gray-haired poet kneeling in a large as·
sembly to kiss the hand of the Sovereign, and one
lady was so moved that she shed tears on the occa·
sion.

Wordsworth now found himself on the full tide

of popularity ; and he had long since ensured a
niche in the Temple of Fame. Though the applause
came slowly, yet it was not too late, and the veteran
poet—almost the last of the great bards of the earlier
half of the century—'bore his blushing honours
thick upon him,' and he was regarded on every side,
not only as an inspired medium, but also as a prophet, commissioned to reveal divine truths to man.
Writing at about this time, De Quincey states :
'Forty-and-seven years it is since William Wordsworth first appeared as an author. Twenty of those
years he was the scoff of the world, and his poetry
a byword of scorn. Since then, and more than
once, senates have rung with acclamations to the
echo of his name. Now, at this moment, whilst
we are talking about him, he has entered upon his
seventy-sixth year. For himself, according to the
course of nature, he cannot be far from his setting ;
but his poetry is but now clearing the clouds that
gathered about its rising. Meditative poetry is,
perhaps, that which will finally maintain most
power upon generations more thoughtful ; and in
this department, at least, there is little competition
to be apprehended by Wordsworth from anything
that has appeared since the death of Shakespeare.'

It was in advanced age that Wordsworth penned
the following noble and touching words to Aubrey
de Vere : 'It is indeed a deep satisfaction to hope
and believe that my poetry will be, while it lasts, a

12—2

help to the cause of virtue and truth, especially
among the young. As for myself, it seems now of
little moment how long I may be remembered.
When a man pushes off in his little boat into the
great seas of infinity and eternity, it surely signifies
little how long he is kept in sight by watchers from
the shore.'

The last few years of Wordsworth's prolonged life
were deeply embittered by sorrow. Writing on the
2 3rd of January, 1846, to his esteemed friend Professor Reed, he says : ' My only surviving brother,
also the late Master of Trinity College, Cambridge,
and an inestimable person, is in an alarming state of
health ; and the only child of my eldest brother,
long since deceased, is now languishing under mortal
illness at Ambleside.' His sister Dorothy had been
a confirmed invalid since 1836. Never very strong,
this sprightly creature had grievously overtaxed her
strength in early life, when she was the constant
companion of the poet in his rambles over hill and
dale, heedless of distance, in all kinds of weather.
Body and mind not unfrequently suffer together,
and it was so in her case. With regard to this distinguished lady, William Howitt says : ' The mind
of that beloved sister has for many years gone, as it
were, before her, and she lives on in a second infancy,
gratefully cherished in the poet's home.' And
Principal Shairp feelingly remarks : ' It is sad to
think that when the world at last knew him

(Wordsworth) for what he was, the great original poet of the century, she who had helped to make him so was almost past rejoicing in it.' Sad indeed was it. It was the will of Providence, however, that she should survive the brother to whom she had been all that the most loving and sympathetic of sisters could be, and probably more than any before her had been. It was not until January, 1855, nearly five years after the poet's death, that

> ' God released her of her pain ;
> And then she went away,'

to regain, as who can question ? the brother of her love, and the many friends who had been removed before her.

On the 2nd of February, 1846, the poet's only surviving brother, Christopher Wordsworth, D.D., the author of ' Ecclesiastical Biography,' several volumes of sermons, and other works, died, in his seventy-second year, and was buried at Buxted, Sussex, of which parish he had for some years been rector.

Early in 1847, on the 20th of January, the poet's younger son, William, was married to the youngest daughter of Reginald Graham, the ceremony taking place at Brighton, where the bride and her family resided.

On the 9th of July, in the same year, to the unutterable grief of Wordsworth, his dearly-beloved daughter, Dora Quillinan, was no more. Her health had been far from satisfactory for some years, and in the spring of 1845 her husband took her to Portugal and Spain for change of scene and air. The benefit derived from the visit, which at first was considerable, proved not to be lasting ; and in the summer of 1847 the crisis occurred. The poet's nephew beautifully says : 'She knew that her end was near, and she looked steadily and calmly at it. None of her natural courage and buoyancy failed her, and it was invigorated and elevated by faith. She gradually declined, and at length her spirit departed, and she fell asleep in peace.' She was laid to rest in Grasmere churchyard. Some conception of the magnitude of the trial experienced by her aged parents on her death, may be inferred from the poet's utterances at this period. 'We bear up,' writes he, 'under our affliction as well as God enables us to do. But, oh ! my dear friend, our loss is immeasurable. God bless you and yours.' And, again, nearly six months after the event, he says : 'Our sorrow, I feel, is for life ; but God's will be done !' It *was* to be for life ; but it was not to be for long.

That the marriage of his darling daughter must have been a fearful wrench to Wordsworth's feelings, notwithstanding his deep attachment to her accomplished husband, is readily apparent from the remarks of Sir Henry Taylor. 'His love for his only daughter,' observes Sir Henry, 'was passionately jealous, and the marriage which was indispensable to her peace and happiness was intolerable to his feelings. The emotions—I may say the throes and agonies of emotion—he underwent were such as an old man could not have endured without suffering in health, had he not been a very strong old man. But he was like nobody else—old or young. He would pass the night, or most part of it, in struggles and storms, to the moment of coming down to breakfast; and then, if strangers were present, be as easy and delightful in conversation as if nothing was the matter. But if his own health did not suffer, his daughter's did, and this consequence of his resistance, mainly aided, I believe, by the temperate but persistent pressure exercised by Miss Fenwick, brought him at length, though far too tardily, to consent to the marriage.'

Henceforth, though the year before his daughter's decease he composed some few pieces, the harp of Wordsworth remained almost incessantly silent. 'At his daughter's death,' says Sir Henry, again, 'a silence, *as* of death, fell upon him; and though during the interval between her death and his own his genius was not at all times incapable of its old animation, I believe it never broke again into song.'

The death of Hartley Coleridge, the eldest son of Samuel Taylor Coleridge, took place on the 6th of January, 1849, and his remains were interred at Grasmere, but a few yards behind the graves of the Wordsworths, to whom he was sincerely attached.

Wordsworth himself selected the spot; and it is said
that he remarked: 'Let him lie by us; he would have
wished it.'   And he added to the sexton: 'Keep the
ground for us—we are old people, and it cannot be
for long.'   The lover of Wordsworth will be reminded of the memorable lines addressed 'To H. C.,
Six Years Old,' in which the poet prophetically
exclaims :

> 'O blessed vision ! happy child !
> Thou art so exquisitely wild,
> I think of thee with many fears
> For what may be thy lot in future years.'

Endowed with a large measure of the genius of his
more illustrious father, Hartley Coleridge greatly
distinguished himself as a Fellow of Oriel College,
Oxford; but it is sad to relate, that, starting aside
like a broken bow, he forfeited the distinction
chiefly owing to his intemperate habits, which clung
to him through life.   His literary career in London
proved unsuccessful for the same reason, as did
also his essay as a schoolmaster at Ambleside.   Un-
stable as water, he could not hope to excel; and his
premature death in his fifty-third year should prove an
unmistakable warning to others.   Still, with all his
faults, he possessed a delightful, amiable disposition,
which endeared him to many.   His love for children
was extraordinary, and he could scarcely pass a
child on the road without passionately taking it in
his arms.   'With hair white as snow,' he had, as
has been well observed, 'a heart as green of May.'

In addition to his poems, he wrote several important works, besides contributing to magazine literature ; but it is as a sonnet writer that he will be longest remembered. His sonnets rank amongst the very finest in the language, many of them being 'gems of purest ray serene,' which are to be met with in every judicious anthology of this charming form of composition. Bearing in mind the sin to which he was, alas ! so prone, we attach a peculiar value to the exquisite sonnet on 'Prayer,' which closes with these noble words :

> 'Pray to be perfect, though material leaven
> Forbid the spirit so on earth to be ;
> But if for any wish thou darest not pray,
> Then pray to God to cast that wish away.'

After all his failures and disappointments in life, however, he sleeps calmly enough now ; and many an admirer of his genius and amiability of character has been deeply affected by reading the inscription on the tombstone of 'the poor inhabitant below :'

> ' BY THY CROSS AND PASSION GOOD LORD DELIVER US.
> HARTLEY COLERIDGE,
> BORN SEPT. 19TH, A.D. 1796 ;
> DECEASED JAN. 6TH, A.D. 1849.'

The sun of Wordsworth's day was now rapidly setting. Although his early literary life had been far from prosperous, yet the tide, as we have seen, had long since turned,

> ' And that which should accompany old age,
> As honour, love, obedience, troops of friends,'

he had looked for, and received in abundance. Wi
the exception of the profound sorrow he experienc
on the removal of so many of his friends, his lat
years were indeed happy and serene—infinite
more so than in the case of most writers. .
virtue is its own reward, so the lot of the po
was, in a manner, bound to be exceptional. The
is something touching and inspiring in the sight
a vessel that has long been the sport of the wav
and the tempests, at length arriving safely a
peacefully at the end of her voyage, and enteri
the haven where she would be; and the put
career of Wordsworth furnishes a striking analo
in these respects. Henceforth there is but little
chronicle, his daily life having been, to a large e
tent, uneventful. 'In 1847, the period of my l
visit,' writes his nephew, 'the course was as follows:
The hour at which the family assembled in t
morning was eight. The day began with praye
as it ended. The form of prayer used was th
compiled from the English and American Liturgi
by Dr. Hook. An intercessory prayer was used f
Miss Wordsworth, who was disabled by sickne
from being present. After breakfast the lessons
the day (morning and evening) were read, and al
the Psalms. Dinner was at two. The final me
was at seven or eight. The intervals between the
meals were filled by walking, writing, reading, a
conversation.'

And now, before the curtain rises on the last act of the drama of the poet's life, let us pause for a few brief moments, and listen to one or two anecdotes, which give us glimpses of Wordsworth as he was in company. The space at our disposal greatly limits our selection.

'At a friend's house, after dinner, the conversation turned upon wit and humour. The author of "Lalla Rookh," who was present, gave some illustrations from Sheridan's "sayings, doings, and writings." Starting from his reverie, Wordsworth said that he did not consider himself to be a witty poet; "indeed," continued he, "I do not think I was ever witty but once in my life."

'A great desire was naturally expressed by all to know what this special drollery was.

'After some hesitation, the old poet said:

'"Well, well, I will tell you. I was standing some time ago at the entrance of my cottage at Rydal Mount. A man accosted me with the question:

'"'Pray, sir, have you seen my wife pass by?"

'"Whereupon I said:

'"'Why, my good friend, I didn't know till this moment that you had a wife!'"

'The company stared, and, finding that the old bard had discharged his entire stock, burst into a roar of laughter, which the facetious Wordsworth, in his simplicity, accepted as a genuine compliment to the brilliancy of his wit.'

We are indebted to Cottle for an amusing story, which is to be found in his life of Coleridge.

'I led my horse to the stable,' he writes, 'where a sad perplexity arose. I removed the harness without difficulty; but after many strenuous attempts I could not remove the collar. In despair, I called for assistance, when Mr. Wordsworth brought his ingenuity into exercise; but after several unsuccessful efforts, he relinquished the achievement as a thing altogether impracticable. Mr. Coleridge now tried his hand, but showed no more skill than his predecessors; for, after twisting the poor horse's neck almost to strangulation and the great danger of his eyes, he gave up the useless task, pronouncing that the horse's head must have grown since the collar was put on; for he said, " it was a downright impossibility for such a huge *os frontis* to pass through so narrow an aperture." Just at this instant a servant-girl came near, and understanding the cause of our consternation, " Ha! master," said she, " you don't go about the work in the right way. You should do like this," when, turning the collar upside down, she slipped it off in a moment, to our great humiliation and wonderment, each satisfied afresh that there were heights of knowledge in the world to which we had not yet attained.'

Barry Cornwall, in his delightful 'Memoir' of Charles Lamb, says :

'Once, at a morning visit, I heard him (Words-

worth) give an account of his having breakfasted
in company with Coleridge, and allowed him to
expatiate to the extent of his lungs.

'"How could you permit him to go on and
weary himself?" said Rogers. "Why, you are to
meet him at dinner this evening!"

'"Yes," replied Wordsworth; "I know that very
well; but we like to take the *sting* out of him
beforehand."'

Wordsworth was dearly attached to Lamb, whose
demeanour to the great poet, says Barry Cornwall,
was 'almost respectful.' But Lamb, 'the frolic and
the gentle,' was a whimsical fellow, and there were
occasions when, in the mirthfulness of his disposition, he forgot himself. Leigh Hunt states, that,
meeting Wordsworth one evening at a friend's
house, Lamb, instead of taking the poet's hand in
the good, old-fashioned, orthodox way, shook him by
the nose, with the greeting, 'How d'ye do, old
Lake Poet?' The contrast between the conduct of
the grave and solemn Wordsworth and that of the
humorous Lamb, was about as wide as it is possible
to imagine, and there is, perhaps, a sly hint at the
gravity of the former conveyed in the following
lines, addressed by Lamb to the poet: 'Some
d——d people have come in,' he writes, 'and I
must finish abruptly. By d——d, I only mean
deuced.'

'Wordsworth and myself,' said Rogers, 'had

walked to Highgate to call on Coleridge, when he was living at Dr. Gillman's. We sat with him two hours; he talking the whole time without intermission. When we left the house we walked for some time without speaking.

' " What a wonderful man he is ! " exclaimed Wordsworth.

' " Wonderful indeed," said I.

' " What depth of thought ! what richness of expression ! " continued Wordsworth.

' " There's nothing like him that ever I heard," rejoined I.

(Another pause.)

' " Pray," inquired Wordsworth, " did you precisely understand what he said about the Kantian philosophy ? "

' Rogers : " Not precisely."

' Wordsworth : " Or about the plurality of worlds ? "

' Rogers : " I can't say I did. In fact, if the truth must out, I didn't understand a syllable from one end of his monologue to the other."

' Wordsworth : " No more did I." '

Poor Coleridge ! ' They fooled thee to the top of thy bent.'

CHAPTER XII.

' 'Tis less than to be born ; a lasting sleep ;
A quiet resting from all jealousy ;
A thing we all pursue. I know besides,
It is but giving over of a game
That must be lost.'

Beaumont and Fletcher.

Wordsworth attends Divine Service at Rydal Chapel for the last time (10th March, 1850)—Is taken ill two days later, and dies in his eighty-first year (23rd April, 1850)—Is interred in Grasmere Churchyard—Inscription on his tombstone—Text of tablet in the church.

WE are now approaching the close of our self-appointed task; and but little remains to be added.

Wordsworth was now an old man, with long locks of silvery hair ; and, like the aged Simeon, he was about to 'depart in peace.' He had been through life blessed with unusually good health, and he had scarcely ever known a day's illness. His chest, however, does not appear to have been very robust, and his writing-desk, he says, was to him ' a place of punishment.'

The words of Shakespeare, put into the mouth of

the faithful Adam, in 'As you like it,' **were**
peculiarly applicable to him :

> 'Though I look old, yet I am strong and lusty ;
> For in my youth I never did apply
> Hot and rebellious liquors in my blood ;
> Nor did not with unbashful forehead woo
> The means of weakness and debility ;
> Therefore my age is as a lusty winter,
> Frosty, but kindly.'

'It is appointed unto men once to die,' however, and Wordsworth's final hour had well-nigh
come.   He had passed his seventy-ninth, and
had nearly completed his eightieth year, when,
on Sunday, the 10th of March, 1850, he attended
Divine Service at Rydal Chapel, as was his wont,
for the last time.   Two days afterwards he walked
towards Grasmere, 'to meet his two nieces,' says his
nephew, 'who were coming from Town End.   He
called at the cottage near the White Moss quarry,
and, the occupant not being within, he sat down on
the stone seat of the porch to watch the setting sun.
It was a cold, bright evening.   His friend and
neighbour, Mr. Roughsedge, came to drink tea at
Rydal ; but Mr. Wordsworth, not being well, went
early to bed.'   It was the beginning of the
end.

This was on the 12th of March ; and, on the 14th,
the patient complained of pain. Medical advice was
obtained from Ambleside. He gradually grew worse,
however, and a few days afterwards the symptoms
became more serious.   The throat, chest, and pleura

were affected. On Sunday, the 7th of April, he attained his eightieth year, and prayer was twice offered on his behalf in Rydal Chapel.

For weeks the Angel of Death, with his ebon wings, kept hovering over the picturesque abode of the poet, dressed in the beauty of the early spring, soon, alas! to be the house of mourning. In the 'Notes' on his transcendent 'Ode on the Intimations of Immortality,' supplied by the poet, he says: 'I used to brood over the stories of Enoch and Elijah, and almost to persuade myself that, whatever might become of others, I should be translated in something of the same way to heaven.' This was uttered without any tinge of vanity. And now, as the end drew nearer day by day, who can doubt that 'the chariot and the horses of fire,' albeit invisible to mortal eye, were in waiting?

On the 20th of the month, the dying poet received the Holy Communion, and 'on or about this day,' says his nephew, 'Mrs. Wordsworth, with a view of letting him know what the opinion of his medical advisers was concerning his case, said gently to him, "William, you are going to Dora." He made no reply at the time, and the words seemed to have passed unheeded; indeed, it was not certain that they had been even heard. More than twenty-four hours afterwards one of his nieces came into the room, and was drawing aside the curtain of his chamber, and then, as if

13

awakening from a quiet sleep, he said, "Is that
Dora ?" '

At length, on the 23rd of the month — the
anniversary of St. George, the patron saint of England, and of Shakespeare's birth and death—the
spirit of the distinguished bard passed away to its
eternal rest. 'God's finger touched him, and he
slept.' Verily, a great man and a prince had that
day fallen—Wordsworth was dead !

The highest authority tells us, that when the
Divine Exemplar died, 'the veil of the temple was
rent in twain from the top to the bottom ; and the
earth did quake, and the rocks rent ; and the
graves were opened ; and many bodies of the
saints which slept arose, and came out of the
graves after His resurrection, and went into the holy
city, and appeared unto many.'

And, in his noble play of ' Hamlet,' Shakespeare
makes one of his characters say :

> ' In the most high and palmy state of Rome,
> A little ere the mightiest Julius fell,
> The graves stood tenantless, and the sheeted dead
> Did squeak and gibber in the Roman streets.'

We are not, in general, inclined to believe in the
supernatural, but we are still less disposed to deny
the occurrence of events which are sufficiently attested, merely because they come not within the
scope of our philosophy. With regard to the death
of Wordsworth, we are not told that even the

ominous raven croaked. But surely it requires little stretch of the imagination to apply the following verses to the eminent prince of song when summoned from the scenes he loved so passing well:

And when at length the poet died,
　　All Nature mourned and hushed her lute ;
　　Even the very birds were mute,
And every gentle zephyr sighed.

Each floweret filled its brilliant eye
　　With dewy tears, and bowed its head ;
　　The sun, dejected, scarcely shed
A gleam of sunshine in the sky.

And in the mountain glens, the wind
　　Chanted a requiem soft and slow,
　　And, moaning sadly to and fro,
Among the rugged passes, pined.

Like human mourners stood the trees,
　　In silence shrouded and in gloom ;
　　Like weepers round an open tomb,
O'ercome with flooding memories.

For one ' was not' whose death had cast
　　A cloud of sadness o'er the land ;
　　And all could see and understand
A mighty power away had passed.

And those who loved his verse in life
　　Found still a greater sweetness there ;
　　Saw it in its perfection rare,
And fed upon its beauties rife.

And tho' to mother earth resigned,
　　He did not *die*, though low he lies ;
　　The bard immortal never dies,
But lives in hearts he leaves behind.

> And thus he won a deathless name
> That Time itself can ne'er efface
> From off the bead-roll of his race,
> And honour in the Hall of Fame.

The entry in the journal kept by Mr. Quillinan, which chronicles the poet's decease, is as follows : ' Mr. Wordsworth breathed his last calmly, passing away almost insensibly, exactly at twelve o'clock, while the cuckoo-clock was striking the hour.'

> ' Death is the crown of life :
> Were death denied, poor men would live in vain ;
> Were death denied, to live would not be life ;
> Were death denied, e'en fools would wish to die.'

Popular as Wordsworth had been during his declining years, he was destined to become yet more noted ; and the circle of his renown is still more and more increasing. Where, during his lifetime, he was read by tens, it is no exaggeration to assert that he is now read by hundreds. Death did for him what it has done for countless others ; it widely ' opened the gate of fame, and shut the gate of envy after it.' He had spent a long, useful, and most honourable career, ' wearing the white flower of a blameless life ;' and may we not say, in the fullest sense of the words : ' He being dead, yet speaketh '?

His remains were lovingly committed to the earth, near those of his children, on Saturday, the 27th of April, in the secluded green churchyard of Grasmere, in presence of a large and deeply-impressed

assemblage of persons.   No poet, perhaps, was ever
buried in a lovelier place, and it is, in his case, peculiarly interesting to know that he himself selected it,
and planted the sombre yew-tree that overshadows
his grave.   The tombstone, which is of the simplest
and most unpretentious character, now bears the
following inscriptions :

> ' William Wordsworth.
> 1850.
> Mary Wordsworth.
> 1859.'

The majestic verse of Milton on Shakespeare,
with the name of Wordsworth substituted for that
of the great poet of all time, will at once suggest
itself to every poetical reader :

> ' What needs my " Wordsworth " for his honoured bones
> The labour of an age in pilèd stones ?
> Or that his hallowed reliques should be hid
> Under a star-ypointing pyramid ?'

' His own prophecy,' says his nephew, ' in the
lines,

> ' " Sweet flower ! belike one day to have
> A place upon thy Poet's grave,
> I welcome thee once more,"

is now fulfilled.   He desired no splendid tomb in a
public mausoleum.   He reposes, according to his
own wish, beneath the green turf, among the dales-
men of Grasmere, under the sycamores and yews of

a country churchyard, by the side of a beautiful stream, amid the mountains which he loved; and a solemn voice seems to breathe from his grave, which blends its tones in sweet and holy harmony with the accents of his poetry, speaking the language of humility and love, of adoration and faith, and preparing the soul, by a religious exercise of the kindly affections, and by a devout contemplation of natural beauty, for translation to a purer, and nobler, and more glorious state of existence, and for a fruition of heavenly felicity.' No utterance could be more appropriate than this.

In the interior of the church, where for so many years the poet had been a worshipper, an elegant marble tablet is to be seen, which bears, above a striking medallion, the accompanying eloquent tribute from the graceful pen of Keble, author of the well-known ' Christian Year :'

' To the Memory of
William Wordsworth,
a true philosopher and poet,

who, by the special gift and calling of Almighty God, whether he discoursed on Man or Nature, failed not to lift up the heart to holy things, tired not of maintaining the cause of the poor and simple ; and so, in perilous times was raised up to be a chief minister, not only of noblest poesy, but of high and sacred truth.

This Memorial
is placed here by his friends and neighbours,
in testimony of respect, affection,
and gratitude.
Anno MDCCCLI.'

The stranger who visits for the first time the
churchyard among the mountains, needs no guide
to conduct him to the poet's lowly grave, a well-
trodden footpath leading to the sacred spot, which
has since become a shrine where thousands upon
thousands resort to muse in silence over the remains of all that was mortal of the great and
illustrious departed, and to pay their ˙adoration to
the undying memory of him—their teacher and
friend—who is so near and dear to many of their
hearts, and who, to his everlasting honour, 'uttered
nothing base,' but rather, in his own exalted
language,

'Made us heirs
Of truth and pure delight by heavenly lays.'

Such, in brief, was the life of Wordsworth.
It forms no part of our duty to deduce any lessons
or moral from it—this we leave the reader to do for
himself.   The history of such a man, if perused in a
proper spirit, cannot fail to impress itself, and make
itself felt, upon every thinking mind.   'Biography,'
says Carlyle, ' is the most universally pleasant, universally profitable of all reading.'   And Longfellow,

with a masterly hand, strikes a true note, in his 'Psalm of Life,' when he sings :

> ' Lives of great men all remind us
>   We can make our lives sublime,
> And, departing, leave behind us
>   Footprints on the sands of time ;
>
> ' Footprints, that perhaps another,
>   Sailing o'er life's solemn main,
> A forlorn and shipwrecked brother,
>   Seeing, shall take heart again.'

CHAPTER XIII.

'The conclusion of the whole matter.'
Ecclesiastes.

On Wordsworth's Poetry.

WE are now to make a few critical observations
on Wordsworth's poetry. And what can we say
that has not already been said, and that, too, over
and over again? Shakespeare tells us, that

> ' To gild refinèd gold, to paint the lily,
> To throw a perfume on the violet,
> To smooth the ice, or add another hue
> Unto the rainbow, or with taper-light
> To seek the beauteous eye of heaven to garnish,
> Is wasteful and ridiculous excess.'

As we are confessedly amongst the rapidly-increasing
number of those that regard the poetry of Wordsworth as 'refined gold,' our object in this chapter
is not so much to 'gild,' as to refer, however briefly
and imperfectly, to some of the most notable
qualities and characteristics of the inestimable mass
of poetic treasure he has for ever bequeathed to
posterity.

The poems of Wordsworth may be roughly divided into three comprehensive classes :—Lyrical Poems, Sonnets, and Blank Verse Compositions. And it may be said, at the outset, that his poetry, great as is its excellence, is, on first acquaintance, by no means as attractive as that of many other poets ; yet the more intimate our knowledge of it becomes, the more it grows upon us. The same may be alleged of some of our grand cathedrals, the external appearance of which gives little promise of the magnificence and delight to be found within the sacred edifices. Wordsworth, as we have stated, is not at first sight prepossessing. There are some lines in ' A Poet's Epitaph ' which, by a general concensus of opinion, have been applied to him by his admirers and critics, as aptly describing his character and disposition :

> ' He is retired as noontide dew,
> Or fountain in a noon-day grove ;
> And you must love him, ere to you
> He will seem worthy of your love.

> ' The outward shows of sky and earth,
> Of hill and valley, he has viewed ;
> And impulses of deeper birth
> Have come to him in solitude.'

His poetic work is not of the sentimental, confectionary style of Tom Moore, but, on the contrary, it is good, pure, and wholesome. There is body and there is life in it ; and we feel as we turn over the pages that we are not so much gathering honey, as laying up a store of more solid, palatable

and lasting food—a food that will not cloy.   To
ourselves it is, and long has been,

> ' A perpetual feast of nectared sweets,
> Where no crude surfeit reigns.'

There are no tinsel accessories in Wordsworth.
All meretricious ornaments, and hackneyed epithets
and phraseology, he discarded, as beneath the dignity
of his art.   He broke away from the house of bondage in which so many of the poets that preceded
him had, for so prolonged a period, been confined as
willing prisoners, and he struck out for a *terra nova* in
poetry—a land of truth and liberty.   He had, in a
pre-eminent degree, what every man that is worth
his salt must possess—the courage of his opinions,
and he did not fail to exercise it, though his per-
sistence in introducing a reform in literature drew
upon him—as it always will—during a long course of
years, the 'envy, hatred, and malice, and all unchari-
tableness' of poetical criticism.   But he turned neither
to the left hand nor to the right.   In the beautiful
language of the poet Gray,

> ' Along the cool sequestered vale of life,
> He kept the noiseless tenor of his way ;'

regardless alike of the perverted judgments of his
critics, and of the chilling receptions accorded to
volume after volume of his poems by the misguided
republic of letters.   He did not conform to the
tenets of his reviewers, and by slow degrees he had

the heartfelt pleasure and satisfaction of finding the literary world coming round to his way of thinking. He was a sufferer, if ever there was one, for the truth ; and he might fittingly have appropriated as his motto, ' *magna est veritas, et prevalebit.*' He was too near the contemporaries of his third, fourth, and fifth decades, to be appreciated at his proper value ; but, as time rolled on, a new generation of unprejudiced readers sprang up, and then—but not till then—it was that he was accepted as a poetical king by the motley multitude of his readers. It is with a great man as with a lofty and imposing mountain ; to see either in all the fulness of its glory, the spectator should not be too close, remembering that no writer ever uttered a more striking thought than Campbell when he sang, that ' distance lends enchantment to the view.' However paradoxical it may appear, the poet who would live, alas ! must die. At all events, death to the bard is the surest way to immortality. There is a certain modicum of truth in the proverb, ' familiarity breeds contempt ;' and there is, unfortunately and ungenerously, a tendency to undervalue the illustrious during their natural lives. It is possible to be too near the light ; and we often travel far to seek that which is to be found at our very feet. The growth of Wordsworth in public estimation has been not unlike that of the oak—slow but sure ; and it now certainly needs no prophet, nor the son of a prophet, to predict that many of his poems will perish only with the wreck of the language in which they are so nobly enshrined. As in the case of Shakespeare, 'he was not of an age, but for all time,' to quote 'rare Ben Jonson;' and his poetry, in general at least, is destined to live. Of much of his work we can truly say, that

> 'Age cannot wither it, nor custom stale
> Its infinite variety.'

It is now nearly forty years since Wordsworth passed beyond the reach of earthly praise or censure, and all narrow jealousy and prejudice being removed, and all false criticism shrouded in oblivion, we can see the poet as he lived—the full measure of the man is revealed to us.

We have said that Wordsworth's poetry may be divided into three classes. We shall take his Lyrical Poems first. The intelligent reader who desires to see the difference between the lyrical verse of Wordsworth and that of his predecessors, has only to compare the two. The result will be a manifest contrast. We do not think, however, that the healthy reform in English poetry was accomplished solely by Wordsworth. Thomson, Cowper, Burns, and Crabbe, before him, had done much to break away from the trammels of the artificial style of poetry, with its common-place, second-hand imagery and description, and turgidity of expression ; but although pioneers—and worthy ones too

—of Wordsworth, they had not worked precisely in the same way. They were poets of a very dissimilar order. Wordsworth, as a poet, stands peculiarly alone. 'None but himself can be his parallel.' It was reserved for him to cleanse the Augean stable of English poetry, and this he effected, with signal success, by the aid of the mighty rivers of simplicity, purity, and truth. In his hands, poetry became a different art altogether; and long before his death he might justly have said : 'The former things are passed away.' It is not too much, but rather a great deal too little, to say, that no man, whether painter or poet, either before or since his time, saw so much in Nature, or invested it with such intense life and spirituality, as Wordsworth. While his youthful contemporary Keats—that divine poet of poets—was ransacking the literature of mythology for subjects for his exquisite and undying poems ; and Byron creating the most imaginative characters by the mere force of his stupendous but, for the most part, misdirected genius ; and Shelley borrowing the materials for his dramas from the classical writers of antiquity ; Wordsworth found enough and to spare in the beauties and common objects of every-day life, which his Muse has sanctified, and over which he has thrown, with the skill of a consummate artist,

> 'The gleam,
> The light that never was on sea or land,
> The consecration, and the poet's dream.'

Wordsworth's early poetry was that of description, but his inherent love of Nature soon led him to that of Man; and it may be questioned whether any poet, ancient or modern, had a finer ear for 'the still, sad music of humanity.' Many of his predecessors may be said to have belonged to those that have ears yet hear not, who have eyes and yet see not; and it was his peculiar privilege to hold a closer and more intimate communion with Nature than any had held before him. He was conspicuously adapted for this by his remarkable poetic insight and mental composition. He himself tells us, that

> ' Minds that have nothing to confer
> Find little to perceive.'

It was 'the vision and the faculty divine,' so largely developed in him, that enabled him to see so much in Nature, which to multitudes is as a sealed book. Coleridge, in his charming Ode, 'Dejection,' brings out this idea forcibly when he sings : 'O Lady ! we receive but what we give.' Nature was to Wordsworth an open volume, which he read as never man read before him. And his sympathies were with what is little, and, to the ordinary mind, unimportant, equally with what is great, and impressive.

> ' To me the meanest flower that blows can give
> Thoughts that do often lie too deep for tears.'

To him Nature was the link that connected earth

with heaven.   According to his philosophy, it **was**
endued with an active principle; and he says,—

> 'I have felt
> A presence that disturbs me with the joy
> Of elevated thoughts ; a sense sublime
> Of something far more deeply interfused,
> Whose dwelling is the light of setting suns,
> And the round ocean and the living air,
> And the blue sky, and in the mind of man :
> A motion and a spirit, that impels
> All thinking things, all objects of all thought,
> And rolls through all things.'

Of many of the lyrical poems of Wordsworth, it
is impossible to speak too highly; they are of the
finest order, both in subject and treatment.   It is
Wordsworth's praise that he is, perhaps, the most
correct of all the great poets, fewer solecisms being
found in his compositions than in those of almost
any other writer. ⋅ He knew the beauty, power, and
pathos of our noble Saxon tongue ; and his writings
pre-eminently constitute a 'well of English,' pure
and undefiled.   He has enriched the language,
moreover, with a large number of new and effective
metres, and it is noticeable that in selecting them
he was singularly happy and successful, suiting
them to the matter he had to convey with extraordinary ability.   What, for example, could be more
appropriate to the beautiful narratives in 'We are
Seven,' 'The Solitude of Binnorie,' 'Ruth,' 'Lucy
Gray,' 'The Horn of Egremont Castle,' 'The Complaint of a Forsaken Indian Woman,' 'Resolution

and Independence,' 'Laodamia,' and many of his other exquisite creations, than the respective metres in which they are written? The charge of puerility and simplicity so frequently advanced against Wordsworth, we need scarcely say, has been grossly exaggerated; though it is undeniable that, in his praiseworthy endeavours to be simple and natural, he occasionally exceeded the narrow line of demarcation which admittedly divides the sublime from the ridiculous. But such lapses are by no means of common occurrence, and we are not sure that we would like these blemishes expurgated. We love Wordsworth so much as he is, with all his faults and imperfections on his head, that he could not be dearer to us without them. There are spots, as all the world knows, in the glorious sun itself; and he that seeks for uniform perfection in science, literature, or art, will have to search for ages, and, at length, give up his quest in despair. If Wordsworth now and then sinks, he does so in distinguished company, for every poet, from the immortal Homer downwards, must at times inevitably nod. But when he soars, he rises calmly, majestically, and gracefully, though he was incapable of prolonged sustained efforts. This inability, however, does not affect his lyrical poems, the brevity of which, in nine cases out of ten, enables him to rise and sustain his flight, descending as skilfully as he ascends. No writer has left behind him a finer

14

body of healthy lyrical work—sufficient to ensure the immortality of a score of princely poets. And the range of his fancy is certainly wide and varied, everything being made subservient to the Muse. In choosing his material, though, doubtless, he did so too exclusively from middle and lower life, we think that he acted wisely ; for has he not enlarged the sympathies, and extended the affections of his readers, to an extent before unknown ? He would have saved himself a large amount of dispraise and obloquy, had he chosen more of his characters from the higher walks in life, and thus have ensured the favour of numbers which was largely and long denied to him. Virtue, like vice, is not confined to any particular class, but is to be found in all. Still, we must 'take the good the gods provide us,' and be thankful. And what a treasury of poetry Wordsworth has given us ! His poems—many of them at least—may fitly be described as 'apples of gold in baskets of silver.' We would have the young in our land well grounded in such of his compositions as are especially suited to them, and thus bestow upon them a legacy worth infinitely more than money. The latter is soon lost, not so the former. We would like to be able to say of many a youth and maiden, in the poet's own language,

> ' Thy mind
> Shall be a mansion for all lovely forms,
> Thy memory be as a dwelling-place
> For all sweet sounds and harmonies ;'

and this could be rendered possible, and largely attained, by their committing to heart, and thus making their own, many of the beautiful and imperishable verses of the great poet-teacher. The space at our disposal necessarily precludes our particularizing the numerous poems, and commenting, ever so briefly, on each; neither is this a task we would willingly impose upon ourselves, our love and veneration for the poet of our choice rendering such a proceeding little short of sacrilege. But we cannot dismiss this part of our subject without insisting on the fact that Wordsworth has given us eyes and ears to see and hear the beauties and sounds in the natural world—both of men and things—around us, which probably we should never have seen and heard, at all events so fully, without him; he has done more to enlist the sensibilities and sympathies of his readers with the joys and sorrows, hopes and fears, pursuits and occupations of the poor, than any poet since the days of Shakespeare, and this, we think, to a larger measure than the Bard of Avon, though the range of the former was limited as compared with that of the latter; he has demonstrated, with the finger of truth, that there are virtues, affection, and true nobility of character in humble life, such as no preceding writer ventured to ascribe to it; he has drawn tightly and enduringly the band which, like a girdle, encircles humanity; and he has conclusively and beautifully shown, that ' one touch of nature makes the whole world kin.' And all this he has effected, more especially in his lyrical poems, though necessarily the same applies in degree to his sonnets, and still more, perhaps, to his noble blank verse compositions.

If Wordsworth is eminent as a lyrical poet, what shall we say of him as a sonnet writer? In this charming form of composition, of which he has given us nearly five hundred examples, he is, we think, perhaps, at his best. He never treads more firmly than in the sonnet, in which his great strength lies, and in which 'he doth bestride the narrow world, like a Colossus.' His finest sonnets may, without exaggeration, be pronounced 'entire and perfect chrysolites,' many of them truly containing 'infinite riches in a little room.' Wordsworth has attained, to our mind, the high distinction of being the greatest sonneteer in the language, not excepting Shakespeare—whose poems of fourteen lines are not sonnets at all, properly so-called—Milton, Keats, Dante Gabriel Rossetti, and Mrs. Browning. And when it is for a moment considered that one faultless sonnet is in itself sufficient to ensure an undying reputation—the case of Blanco White, who will go down to posterity as the author of ' Night,' may be cited in proof of this—what a glorious and overwhelming immortality has not Wordsworth achieved! We do not hesitate to say, that more sonnets of superlative excellence, both as regards thought and execution, which could less be spared than any in the whole compass of sonnet literature, can be culled from Wordsworth, than from any other writer. 'The prison unto which he doomed himself' in the sonnet, was to him abundantly large; in it he found 'ample room and verge enough.' His two well-known sonnets on the sonnet are delightful conceptions; and his poems of this class generally may justly be characterized as

> 'Jewels . . . . .
> That on the stretched forefinger of all time
> Sparkle for ever.'

His sonnets dedicated to National Independence and Liberty are unquestionably amongst the finest, if not, in many instances, the very finest outbursts of ennobling enthusiasm and patriotism ever uttered by man, many of them stirring the soul of the reader 'like the sound of a trumpet.' Such, for example, is the memorable one in which occur the inspiring words :

> 'We must be free or die, who speak the tongue
> That Shakespeare spake; the faith and morals hold
> Which Milton held.'

And such another is the glowing address 'To the Men of Kent. October, 1803,' commencing,

> 'Vanguard of Liberty, ye men of Kent.'

England, be it remembered, was then dreading an invasion by the French, and men's hearts were

failing them for fear. Let this martial sonnet be
read aloud. The sestet, or last six lines, is magnificent :

> 'Left single, in bold parley, ye, of yore,
> Did from the Norman win a gallant wreath ;
> Confirmed the charters that were yours before ;—
> No parleying now ! In Britain is one breath ;
> We all are with you now from shore to shore :—
> Ye men of Kent, 'tis victory or death !'

We are not slow to award to Wordsworth the foremost place as a sonnet writer. In our estimation,
he has written the noblest sonnets in the English—or
in any other—language. Few impartial judges can, we
think, deny this. At all events, Wordsworth, when
he is at his best in the sonnet, has but few, if any
equals, and no superiors. Where are they ? He
was peculiarly at home in this form of poem, which
he made the vehicle of his opinions on a wide multi-
plicity of subjects, giving ' timely utterance ' to his
thoughts not unfrequently in splendid verse, which
the world assuredly will not willingly let die. In
his sonnets, which are the very antipodes to the
' language really used by men,' the poet enriching
them with all the wealth of a copious and brilliant
vocabulary, and polishing them to the fullest extent
of his power, we can see him as in a mirror; not
only the matter, but the manner also, of many of
them leaving nothing to be desired. He knew what
he had to say, and he said it. There is no prolixity
or tediousness—whatever may be urged against some

of his longer poems in those respects—in the sonnets;
indeed, no writer has ever expressed himself with
more compactness, directness, and lucidity, than
Wordsworth in these charming compositions, the
best of which may aptly be compared to a pellucid
stream meandering sweetly on its course, in which
the very pebbles are discernible to every eye ; or to
a well of transparent water, through which we can
see clearly to the bottom. The secret of Wordsworth's success in the sonnet is possibly not far to
seek, inasmuch as, with an intensely poetical mind,
inclined at times to be too diffuse and exhaustive,
he was confined in the expression of his 'soul-
animating strains' to a prescribed limit. He himself
says,—

> ' In sundry moods, 'twas pastime to be bound
> Within the sonnet's scanty plot of ground ;
> Pleased if some souls (for such there needs must be)
> Who have felt the weight of too much liberty,
> Should find brief solace there, as I have found.'

We come now to Wordsworth's Blank Verse
Compositions. He had a marvellous ear for this—
the most difficult of all kinds of poetry. If we
except Shakespeare, Milton, and Akenside when
most inspired, Wordsworth is, *par excellence,* the
greatest master of blank verse in the language. He
has given us passages, almost without number, which
even Milton might well envy ; and what higher
praise can be accorded ? To say that he is unequal,
is, in other words, to assert that he was but human.

Man is not perfect. But it is alleged, that, not only
in 'The Prelude,' a work of his comparatively
earlier life, but also in 'The Excursion,' his greatest
achievement, there are numerous 'weary, stale, flat,
and unprofitable' passages, unredeemed by any of
the graces or flowers of poetry. Strange as it may
appear, this is but the case. The truth is that
Wordsworth, more especially in blank verse, is
unduly prone to be too didactic and diffuse; 'he
draweth out the thread of his verbosity finer than
the staple of his argument'—a very fatal error in
poetry, which, to be good, must necessarily be more
suggestive than *expressive.* Something must be left
to the reader's imagination, else the charm is gone.
Prolixity is out of place in all poetical forms of composition. Wordsworth knew this as well as any-
body ; but, nevertheless, the fact remains that there
is extreme diffuseness occasionally in both of the
poems referred to. But when we have stated this,
we have said the worst. What remains is mostly
verse of remarkable quality, such as only a great
master—a very prince of song—could have produced.
It would be impossible in these pages to refer to many
of the most admired passages ; we must, therefore,
content ourselves with briefly referring the reader
to the first two books of 'The Excursion,' which
contain the beautifully-pathetic episode of Margaret
and the Ruined Cottage, and the magnificent description of a glorious spectacle upon the mountains ;

to the charming account of the Chaldean, Grecian, and other modes of belief, in the fourth book ; to the exquisite narrative of the Churchyard among the Mountains, in the sixth and seventh books ; and to the inimitable word-painting of the ram by the side of a rivulet, in the ninth book :

> ' By happy chance we saw
> A two-fold image ; on a grassy bank
> A snow-white ram, and in the crystal flood
> Another and the same !   Most beautiful,
> On the green turf, with his imperial front
> Shaggy and bold, and wreathèd horns superb,
> The breathing creature stood ;'

and so on.   No finer strains of the kind are to be found in the whole range of poetry.   They are roses without thorns, that will never lose their sweetness.   Of 'The Excursion,' may not all true lovers of Wordsworth exclaim, with Valentine, in 'The Two Gentlemen of Verona,' that they are

> ' As rich in having such a jewel,
> As twenty seas, if all their sands were pearl,
> The water nectar, and the rocks pure gold ' ?

'The Excursion' is probably the finest poem of the nineteenth century.   We envy the enjoyment of the poetical individual who is about to make a maiden perusal of it, though we are fully persuaded that, like sterling friendship, it improves upon better acquaintance.   To us it certainly does.   We can at all times turn to its pages with unalloyed pleasure and we invariably rise refreshed and strengthened by these rests by the way.

'The Prelude,' which is an autobiographical poem, in which Wordsworth traces the growth of his own mind, should be read and re-read by every poetical reader. It is not, of course, without considerable defects, but it abounds with innumerable beauties of the highest degree of excellence. The work, which was addressed to Coleridge, was commenced in the beginning of the year 1799, when the poet and his sister quitted Goslar on their return to England, and completed in the summer of 1805. It consists of fourteen books, and must ever be regarded as a permanent memorial of the poet's transcendent genius. Space forbids our attempting to give an epitome of this unrivalled history; we cannot, therefore, do better than advise our readers, one and all, to peruse it for themselves. Those who now read it for the first time on this recommendation, will be everlastingly thankful for being directed to such a mine of pure and imperishable poetry.

Of Wordsworth's shorter blank verse compositions, it is easier to speak, as they are more widely known. 'The Brothers' is undoubtedly one of the most beautiful and pathetic idyllic poems in the language. 'Vaudracour and Julia' is a charming narrative, yielding, alas! for it is founded in fact, another striking proof that 'the course of true love never did run smooth.' 'Michael' is a sad pastoral, feelingly and powerfully

written; indeed, few more touching stories have
ever been conceived. 'Nutting,' 'There was a Boy,'
'Tintern Abbey,' 'The Old Cumberland Beggar,'
and many other pieces, are sparkling gems in the
poet's diadem; and poor would we be without them.
We are assured that new readers, after a perusal
of the poems referred to, will thank us for thus
bringing them under their notice, and that those
best acquainted with them will cheerfully endorse
every word we have uttered with regard to them.

With reference to Wordsworth's general poetical
writings, if any evidence of his pre-eminence as a
poet were needed, it is to be abundantly found in
the widespread influence he has had on many of his
contemporaries, and on almost every one of his
numerous successors, Byron, Keats, Shelley, Tennyson, Browning, Buchanan, Matthew Arnold, Henry
Taylor, Bryant, Longfellow, and others. A double
portion of his spirit seems to have been bestowed on.
Ruskin, the great apostle of the Wordsworthian
philosophy.

Wordsworth's love for flowers, stars, and all the
many varied beauties of Nature, was strongly characteristic of him, and also of a greater poet-teacher than
he, who spake as never man spake, and who bade
us 'consider the lilies . . . how they grow!'

No poet scarcely has given us more

> 'Thoughts whose very sweetness yieldeth proof
> That they were born for immortality,'

than Wordsworth. Coleridge remarked to him, 'Since Milton I know of no poet with so many *felicities* and unforgettable lines and stanzas as you.' His early theory of poetic diction was right in part, but wrong, we think, in the main, as a reference to the great majority of his own poems sufficiently proves. It must be admitted that notably in his sonnets, 'The Excursion,' and most of his later poems, including his odes, his diction is, in general, in direct conflict with that of the 'Lyrical Ballads,' the most gorgeous and scholarly language being employed with conspicuous success and effect. It cannot, therefore, be doubted that, to a large extent, his early poetical theory was a conceit of his youth, which in maturer years he had the wisdom to cast aside. We cannot, however, if we would, acquit him of the charge of incongruity, so commonly brought against him, of which several instances are to be found in his writings. The exalted language of the Pedlar, in 'The Excursion,' and that of the aged Leech Gatherer, in 'Resolution and Independence,' may be mentioned as examples of this. Nevertheless, we would not have him other than what he is.

A word as to his Pantheism. Once it is understood that he was a *teacher*, not a *preacher*, the case falls to the ground. He believed that it was not the province of the bard to intrude unduly into sacred things—whether he was right or wrong, we care not to inquire—hence the reason that he has been assailed by some short-sighted critics as a non-Christian poet. But if there is not excessive Christianity, there is abundant Catholicity in his writings. Truth is many-sided; and, in treating a subject poetically, he not unfrequently brought out but one aspect of it, leaving the rest to the preacher. Who but a Christian author could have penned such noble lines as these ?—

> ' Oh ! there is never sorrow of heart
> That shall lack a timely end,
> If but to God we turn, and ask
> Of Him to be our Friend !'
> *The Force of Prayer.*

And, again :

> ' But when the great and good depart
> What is it more than this—
>
> That man, who is from God sent forth,
> Doth yet again to God return ?—
> Such ebb and flow must ever be,
> Then wherefore should we mourn ?'
> *Loud is the Vale.*

Let the reader peruse, amongst other poems too numerous to mention, ' Not seldom Clad in Radiant Vest,' and ' The Labourer's Noon-day Hymn,' to say nothing of ' The Excursion,' and he will at once see for himself that no truer Christian, perhaps, ever lived. His life was an epistle ' known and read of all men.'

In his various Pastoral Poems, and indeed in all his descriptive pieces, Wordsworth treads on *terra firma.* The beautiful district in which he resided for so long, he knew intimately, as a devoted lover knows his mistress ; and in his poetry

> ' He murmurs near the running brooks
> A music sweeter than their own '—

a music that will echo and re-echo, not only down the rolling ages of time, but of eternity also.

It need scarcely be added, after what we have said, that Wordsworth is the poet of purity. He ' uttered nothing base.' There is not an indelicate thought or expression in the whole of his writings, which—and this is high praise—can be implicitly placed in the hands of the youngest reader, and of the most modest and sensitive maiden. He was truly able to say, that 'none of his works, written since the days of his early youth, contained a line that he should wish to blot out, because it pandered to the baser passions of our nature.' He is, however, too profound, meditative, and introspective for many, if not most, of his readers, and not sufficiently sensuous for the masses, with whom, accordingly, he will never, we think, be excessively popular as a poet.

' Poetry,' says Wordsworth, 'is as immortal as the heart of man.' Unquestionably his own is ; and it may safely be predicted that much of it will endure as long as the language it so nobly adorns. The poetical fabric which he constructed is erected upon the rock of truth, the only safe foundation.

And now to 'gather up the fragments that remain, that nothing be lost,' let us consider what Wordsworth has done for us. Amongst many other lessons, he has taught us:

> 'Never to blend our pleasure or our pride,
> With sorrow of the meanest thing that feels;'

that

> 'There is
> One great society alone on earth:
> The noble living and the noble dead;'

that

> 'Soft is the music that would charm for ever;
> The flower of sweetest smell is shy and lowly;'

that—the poet-teacher is addressing a child—

> 'Small service is true service while it lasts:
> Of humblest friends, bright creature! scorn not one:
> The daisy, by the shadow that it casts,
> Protects the lingering dew-drop from the sun;'

that

> 'Wisdom is ofttimes nearer when we stoop
> Than when we soar;'

and, finally, for 'of making many "quotations" there is no end,' he has shown us, like an inspired apostle, that

> 'The primal duties shine aloft, like stars;
> The charities that soothe, and heal, and bless,
> Are scattered at the feet of Man, like flowers.'

This, and infinitely more, he has impressed upon us. He has been his own prophet; and his noble words with reference to his poems, the destiny of which he trusted was 'to console the afflicted; to add sunshine to daylight, by making the happy happier ; to teach the young and the gracious of every age to see, to think, and feel, and, therefore, to become more actively and securely virtuous,' are daily being fulfilled throughout the civilized world.

It will readily be seen that our estimate of Wordsworth is a high one. He was not only the greatest poet of his generation, but also since the days of

> 'That mighty orb of song,
> The divine Milton,'

by whose side it needs slight exercise of the imagination to fancy him sitting, together with Spenser, Shakespeare, and other immortal bards, in the bright Elysian fields. That his station in English literature may now be regarded as fixed and permanent, there would appear to be but little room to doubt, since it seems inconceivable for him to be surpassed. Still, we cannot foresee what poetry may have before it in the future ; it may be that, like science, it is yet comparatively in its infancy. We are not agreed with Lord Macaulay, that 'as civilization advances, poetry almost necessarily declines,' the poetical achievements of the Victorian era affording a conclusive proof to the contrary. True poetry may well be regarded as a mirror which gives a faithful reflection of the different ages in which we live ; and the best poetry, in a measure, is, perhaps, that which comes nearest to the realization of this ideal.

If a Golden Age in society were about to dawn upon mankind, what a glorious era of poetry would there be in store for us ! Meanwhile, Wordsworth, having accomplished his exalted mission, and attained one of the highest Alpine peaks in the abiding land of song, remains there, and it is unlikely, so far as we can judge, that his place will ever be justly challenged.

In taking a lingering leave of our subject, we are conscious that we have but ill discharged our self-imposed undertaking, still,

> ' 'Tis done ; 'tis numbered with the things o'erpast ;
> Would that it were to come !'

In conclusion, we can find no more appropriate words than these of Beaumont and Fletcher, which might well be inscribed on any effigy of William Wordsworth, the poet of Man, of Nature, and of Human Life :

> ' Nothing can cover his high fame, but Heaven ;
> No pyramids set off his memories,
> But the eternal substance of his greatness ;
> To which we leave him.'

THE END.

Elliot Stock, Paternoster Row, London.

Printed in Great Britain
by Amazon